Praise for *The Self-Driven Child*

"Instead of trusting kids with choices . . . many parents insist on micromanaging everything from homework to friendships. For these parents, Stixrud and Johnson have a simple message: Stop. Instead of thinking of yourself as your child's boss or manager, try *consultant*."
—NPR

"William Stixrud and Ned Johnson focus on the ways that children today are being denied a sense of controlling their own lives—doing what they find meaningful, and succeeding, or failing, on their own. Screen time, the authors say, is part of the problem, but so are well-meaning parents and schools, who are unwittingly taking from children the opportunities they need to grow stronger, more confident, and more themselves."
—*Scientific American*

"If there's one book I'd recommend to parents who are raising children of all ages—I'm talking preschool to 12th grade—this is the book."
—*Atomic Moms*

"In trying too hard to control their children, too often parents have unwittingly become part of the problem they're trying to solve. Combining deep insights from clinical practice and educational coaching, Stixrud and Johnson have written a penetrating account of the chronic problems that many families now face and an incisive, practical guide to what parents can do to relieve them . . . An essential book for parents and educators everywhere."
—Sir Ken Robinson, PhD, educator, and
New York Times bestselling author of *Creative Schools*

"If you still have questions about whether or not excessive pressure and a narrow version of success are truly harming our children, *The Self-Driven Child* is an absolute must-read. While most books on the impact of stress on child development offer anecdotes and clinical examples, Stixrud and Johnson make it clear that it is now *research* that explains why kids don't thrive under our current priorities. A healthy child needs a healthy brain. Not only do they produce the evidence that shows why unremitting achievement pressure is toxic to our children, they also show us what the alternative would look like. It is not an overstatement to say that this is one of the most radical and important books on raising healthy, resilient, purpose-driven kids."
—Madeline Levine, PhD, author of
The Price of Privilege and *Teach Your Children Well*

"Compelling, revolutionary, and wise, *The Self-Driven Child* empowers parents with the courage, the tools, and the mindset to reduce toxic stress, and to foster our child's capacity for resilience, success, and optimal development. Its message—that we should trust kids to have more control over their own lives—is one every parent needs to hear."
—Tina Payne Bryson, PhD, coauthor of
The Whole Brain Child and *The Yes Brain*

"Sometimes the most helpful thing we can do as parents is to parent our children a little less. This humane, thoughtful book turns the latest brain science into valuable practical advice for parents on how to pull back, when to engage, and when to let go. Read it. Your children will thank you."
—Paul Tough, *New York Times* bestselling author of
How Children Succeed

"This serious and probing look at how to give our children the right kinds of independence shows us how much power we have to ensure they can function optimally. It is a book about how to make our children more meaningfully independent, and to set ourselves free in the process."
—Andrew Solomon, author of *Far from the Tree*

"*The Self-Driven Child* will guide parents to the sweet spot between helicopter and hands-off parenting. Stixrud and Johnson ground their clear and practical advice in cutting-edge research and years of experience working with young kids and teens. An invaluable resource for the thinking parent."
—Lisa Damour, PhD, author of *Untangled*

"A battleplan to attack the anxiety that's devouring kids and decimating their native potential, this extraordinary book shines a light into the darkness of test dread, chronic sleeplessness, 24/7 social-media 'beauty pageants' and the full array of stress-induced forces that undermine children. But Stixrud and Johnson do more than identify the demons—they slay them. Read this incisive, witty, deeply-researched book and help your child bend toward the sunlight of learning and self-directed joy. A must-read."
—Ron Suskind, Pulitzer Prize–winning journalist
and author of *Life, Animated*

"Stixrud and Johnson combine science and compassion to make the case that parental over-control is eroding our kids' confidence, competence and mental health. Accessible, compelling and richly researched, *The Self Driven Child* reveals the clear links between the stresses of competitive schooling and the anxiety and depression that are so widespread in kids today. This urgently-needed book has the potential to revolutionize the way we parent."

—Judith Warner, author of *A Perfect Madness:*
Motherhood in the Age of Anxiety

"Remember all the time you spent doing something just for fun and it wasn't a class or an organized sport? No grades? No trophies? That turns out to be what kids need to succeed. 'Self-driven' time."

—Lenore Skenazy, author of *Free Range Kids*

"As parents we wonder, 'How can I help my kids learn to make good decisions?' This lucidly written, deeply insightful, and highly engaging book—the best parenting book I've read in a long time—takes the mystery out of that process. All the chapters—on why a sense of control is so important for kids, how to help kids develop their inner drive, the need to tame technology, and how you can teach even young children to understand and influence the working of their brain—give you the science behind the authors' recommendations and action steps you can immediately take in your family. We learn what good guidance looks like: how to help kids make thoughtful choices, handle stress, and grow in confidence so that they can positively affect the course of their lives. As Stixrud and Johnson make crystal clear, raising a 'self-driven' child doesn't mean doing less as a parent; it actually means doing more—but in a collaborative, mutually respectful relationship that's more rewarding for both parent and child. You'll still be a critically important authority figure but also a consultant who asks questions like 'What's your Plan B if Plan A doesn't work out?' You'll be a parent who helps your child develop what the Greeks considered the master virtue: good judgment. That's a gift that will last a lifetime."

—Thomas Lickona, PhD, author of
Character Matters and *How to Raise Kind Kids*

"This is the book we've all been waiting for. As a psychologist specializing in anxiety and stress in children, I have witnessed firsthand the fundamental change that children experience once they learn to face their fears and find the inner drive to take charge of their lives. The resulting sense of agency is transformative, and stays with them. This book offers solid and clear advice on how to create opportunities for our children to discover their own drive and develop that internal locus of control that is necessary to thrive in adulthood. More than ever, parents need the clarity and guidance so effectively expressed in *The Self-Driven Child*. Each chapter ends with a summary called 'What to Do Tonight,' which explains how to apply the information in a practical and relatable way. This book will give parents much-needed insights into the child's experience and how to facilitate the very best conditions to set them up for a rewarding and successful future."

—Bonnie Zucker, PsyD, author of
Anxiety-Free Kids and *Take Control of OCD*

Praise for *What Do You Say?*

"A nuanced and enormously insightful look into the struggles facing so many children and teens . . . A wonderful resource for contemporary parenting, this title should knock less relevant child-raising guides right off the shelf."   —*Booklist*

"Stixrud and Johnson provide compassionate, well-supported suggestions and strategies for parents to help their kids deal with ever-more-competitive academics and extracurriculars. The authors make a highly persuasive case for how parents can help their children segue from feeling stressed and powerless to feeling loved, trusted, and supported."   —*Publishers Weekly*

"In an age when childhood anxiety, depression, and suicide are on the rise, parents need, more than ever, tools for communicating effectively with children. *What Do You Say?* could not have arrived at a better time and is essential reading for today's parents."   —*Booklist*

"Full of easy-to-implement tips, this is a resource parents will return to."   —*Publishers Weekly* (starred review)

"A must-read for any parent who finally wants to stop arguing, bickering, and negotiating with their kids but who also wants their children to succeed and do well in life. Stixrud and Johnson provide clear, actionable guidance on how to motivate kids to do well in school, to conquer their fears and anxieties, and ultimately to pursue activities that bring joy and happiness. The advice in this book has already helped me become a kinder, more effective mom."

—Michaeleen Doucleff, *New York Times*
bestselling author of *Hunt, Gather, Parent*

PENGUIN LIFE

THE SEVEN PRINCIPLES FOR RAISING A SELF-DRIVEN CHILD

William R. Stixrud, PhD, is a clinical neuropsychologist and founder of The Stixrud Group, as well as a faculty member at Children's National Medical Center and an assistant professor of psychiatry and pediatrics at the George Washington University School of Medicine. He has authored numerous articles and book chapters on topics related to the adolescent brain, stress, sleep deprivation, and meditation.

Ned Johnson is an educator, tutor, and parent. President and "tutor-geek" of PrepMatters, an educational company providing academic tutoring and standardized test preparation, Ned is a battle-tested veteran of test prep, stress regulation, and optimizing student performance. Ned has spent roughly fifty-thousand hours helping students one-on-one conquer an alphabet of standardized tests, learn to manage their anxiety, and develop their own motivation to succeed. Ned is the host of the *The Self-Driven Child* podcast, on which he digs into conversation with parenting and education experts.

Bill and Ned are coauthors of the national bestselling book, *The Self-Driven Child*, which is published in nineteen countries and eighteen languages. It has sold more than 800,000 copies worldwide. They have also coauthored an acclaimed second book, *What Do You Say? Talking with Kids to Build Motivation, Stress Tolerance, and a Happy Home*.

Bill and Ned's work has been featured in media outlets such as NPR, CNN, MSNBC, ABC News, *The New York Times*, *The Washington Post*, *The Times of London*, *The Wall Street Journal*, *U.S. News and World Report*, *Time Magazine*, *Scientific American*, *Business Week*, *Barron's*, and *New York Magazine*.

ALSO BY WILLIAM STIXRUD, PHD, AND NED JOHNSON

What Do You Say? How to Talk with Kids to Build Motivation, Stress Tolerance, and a Happy Home

The Self-Driven Child: The Science and Sense of Giving Your Kids More Control Over Their Lives

The
Seven Principles
for Raising *a*
Self-Driven Child

A Workbook

William Stixrud, PhD, *and* Ned Johnson

life

PENGUIN BOOKS
An imprint of Penguin Random House LLC
1745 Broadway, New York, NY 10019
penguinrandomhouse.com

A Penguin Life Book

Set in Baskerville MT Pro with Benton Sans Pro

Designed by Sabrina Bowers

LIBRARY OF CONGRESS CATALOGING-IN-PUBLICATION DATA
Names: Stixrud, William R., author. | Johnson, Ned, 1970– author.
Title: The seven principles for raising a self-driven child: a workbook /
William Stixrud, PhD, and Ned Johnson.
Description: [New York] : Penguin Books, [2025] |
Includes bibliographical references and index.
Identifiers: LCCN 2024043964 (print) | LCCN 2024043965 (ebook) |
ISBN 9780143138259 (trade paperback) | ISBN 9780593512401 (ebook)
Subjects: LCSH: Child rearing. | Parent and child. | Motivation (Psychology) in children.
Classification: LCC HQ769.S82155 2025 (print) | LCC HQ769 (ebook) |
DDC 649/.1—dc23/eng/20241226
LC record available at https://lccn.loc.gov/2024043964
LC ebook record available at https://lccn.loc.gov/2024043965

Printed in the United States of America
1st Printing

The authorized representative in the EU for product safety and compliance is Penguin
Random House Ireland, Morrison Chambers, 32 Nassau Street, Dublin D02 YH68,
Ireland, https://eu-contact.penguin.ie.

BILL

To the parents, educators, and mental health professionals in the U.S. and around the world who have taken the time to tell us how giving their kids, their students, and their clients more control has transformed relationships and improved lives. Their feedback makes me wish I had twenty-five more years to do this work!

NED

To all the parents who, for more than thirty years, have trusted us to work with their children—their greatest treasure—and to all those wonderful kids, teens, and young adults. From you, we have learned so, so much about how people think, learn, grow, and thrive, helping us become better educators, parents, and people. We are endlessly grateful.

Contents

INTRODUCTION:
How to Use the
Seven Principles

A **couple of years ago** we noticed that the same woman kept attending our talks, which we have given regularly to thousands of parents and educators. She seemed to listen attentively, took copious notes, and asked good questions. Our script isn't that different from one talk to another, so we were curious about why she kept showing up. Was she a talent scout? A competitor looking to start her own series of talks? After we saw her at a fourth lecture, we simply decided to ask her: "Why do you keep coming to hear us?"

"I always leave your talks feeling so calm," she explained. "Like it's safe to trust my kid and to not feel that I have to be on him all the time. But then something will happen—he'll lie to me, or screw something up, or I'll feel pressure from another parent who mentions how their kid did on a big math test I didn't even know about, or I'll get pressure from my kid's teacher—and I am back to being panicked."

We were her version of a "calm" button. It made sense. Our core message is that kids do better when they have a sense of control over their lives. Although it's a message that's supported by hundreds of scientific studies, the guidance sometimes feels counterintuitive to parents, and counterintuitive to the culture we live in—in which parents are expected to control their kids. The problem with this expectation, however (and this is one of the most profound things we have learned about children—and about people in general), is that you can't make them do things against their will. You can't force an infant to stop crying, a defiant child to do schoolwork, or a teenager to break up with a boyfriend she insists she loves, which means that you really can't control them. And the fact that we can't actually *make* them bend to our wishes—even if we are just trying to protect them from failure or pain—means that it couldn't be our responsibility to make sure our kids always behave well in public, do their homework every night, do their best every time, make decisions that we agree with, or turn out a certain way. Coming to terms with our lack of control is the first step toward feeling that it's safe and right to give up what doesn't work and to find more successful ways of motivating, encouraging, and persuading our kids.

If you haven't read our work before, know that every bit of advice in this book and our previous books, *The Self-Driven Child* and *What Do You Say?*, is based on the latest research in psychology, neuroscience, and education, as well as sixty-five years of combined experience working with children, teens, and young adults. Decades of research on the importance of a sense of control for mental health and internal motivation— and on the problems associated with parental overcontrol— support our own experience that kids turn out better if their parents treat them respectfully and are *not* overly controlling. This is, in part, because a low sense of control is the most stressful thing we can experience, and an absence of agency contributes strongly to all of the stress-related mental health problems affecting young people, including anxiety disorders, depression, eating and substance use disorders, and self-harm. The U.S. Surgeon General recently referred to the current status of adolescent mental health as "the defining public health crisis of our lifetime," and younger and younger children are developing anxiety disorders and major depressive disorders—and are being admitted to hospitals for suicidal thinking. The *financial and emotional costs of the current levels of anxiety and unhappiness in young people are enormous.* And the foothold that will help us climb our way back to firmer, healthier ground is nurturing and making space for a sense of control.

So often serious problems are actually symptoms of a low sense of control. We treat the symptoms, and rightly so, but we also need to look at the bigger picture. If you're engaging in self-harm or have an eating or substance use disorder, you're trying to get some control over emotional pain that feels uncontrollable. If you're anxious, your thinking feels out of control; you'd like to stop worrying but you can't. If you're depressed, life feels overwhelming and uncontrollable, and it's hard to get out of bed. The common denominator in all of these is pretty clear. In our experience, nothing good happens when kids (or their parents) have a low sense of control, such as when they feel helpless, hopeless, stuck, or resigned—or are chronically pressured, obsessively driven, and/or exhausted.

We think of a sense of control in two dimensions, *subjective* and *physiological*. Subjectively, when you have a sense of control, you have a strong sense of autonomy, and you feel confident that you can cope with the challenges that come your way. Physiologically, to experience a sense of control your brain's prefrontal cortex (which mediates the executive functions) needs to regulate the amygdala (the brain's "threat detector") and the rest of the body's stress response system.

The more recently evolved prefrontal cortex is able to think clearly, to consider the past and the future, to put things into perspective, and to calm yourself down when you start to feel stressed. The much more primitive amygdala, on the other hand, simply senses and reacts to any perceived threat. So, when you're operating from the prefrontal cortex, you're more thoughtful, focused, clearheaded, goal-directed, and emotionally resilient—and life feels under control and manageable—because the brain works more efficiently and effectively.

These findings are true for kids, adolescents and adults, young and old. (They are also true for primates, dogs, and rodents!) However, a sense of control is particularly important during the brain's formative years. The brain develops more between the ages of twelve and eighteen than at any other time in life, except for the first few years. High anxiety and/or depression experienced in adolescence appear to "scar" the brain, making that brain more vulnerable to anxiety and/or depressive episodes later in life. For example, if teenagers become depressed, they will be more vulnerable to insomnia, pessimism, and to feeling a lower level of enjoyment from positive experiences than they did before, even after they start to feel better. This will place them at higher risk for depression than they would have been otherwise. Although some experts attribute this increased risk factor in young adults to very real cultural factors such as decreased job prospects, the enormous cost of housing, college pressure and college debt, and so forth, we suspect that anxious and stressed adolescents are more likely to become adults who don't as easily cope with life's challenges. For this reason, mental health experts emphasize the importance of *preventing* mental health problems in young people.

Increasing a sense of control is also one of the most powerful ways of *treating* mental health problems in children, teens, and adults. According to some recent studies, the main reason that cognitive behavioral therapy helps young people who are struggling with anxiety, depression, or trauma to feel and do better is that it increases their sense of control. It helps them gain control over their negative thinking, learn to regulate their stress response, and have the experience of handling things that used to make them panic. Recent studies have also shown that one of the main reasons sleep, exercise, and meditation promote mental health is that we feel a stronger sense of control when we're well rested, after we've deeply relaxed our minds and bodies, and after we've "blown off" stress through exercise.

Studies also show us that a healthy sense of control is crucial for developing the self-motivation that we want to nurture in kids. For kids to be self-motivated, they must have a sense that this is *their* life, that they can solve problems through their own efforts, and that they aren't simply jumping through hoops or doing things to get a reward or avoid punishment. In other words, they need to have a sense of control.

So why don't parents operate in ways that encourage their child's autonomy? If the science is that clear, and the consequences of *not* supporting autonomy are potentially dire, why isn't this guidance baked into our culture? Haven't we generally evolved as a species in ways that serve us? Isn't this one such way? The reason is that encouraging a sense of control can be hard for parents—and for educators; the more we sit on our hands, zip our lips, and support a child's autonomy, the less control—and the more stress—*we* experience. Compounding the problem, we are also bombarded by constant messages that stoke fear. Right when we *think* we have achieved parental calm, another article is published about the perils of technology for adolescent brains, or another parent makes small talk about how few students pass AP Chemistry, or a teacher informs us that our son has failed to turn in his homework—even though we've told the teacher time and time again to bring it up with *him*. The best way most of us know to combat fear is to seize control: *This crazy ride is scary and uncertain, but look—we've got hold of the reins!*

For you parents who are trying to walk the path of raising a self-driven child against the headwinds of a culture that tells you to seize control, this book is for you. This book is for that mom who kept showing up at our lectures, and for the hundreds of parents we've met just like her, including the mother of a child in a highly competitive high school who recently asked us to help her and her friends "get off the crazy train." Many parents *know* that their behavior isn't helping—it's just really hard to shift to another way of being.

While we know that readers have learned a lot from our previous books and many other sources that encourage kids' autonomy, we also know that our core messages require some reinforcement, and that parents and educators are *busy*. They need some quick shots of courage, and permission to trust in a world that constantly seems to undermine that trust. They also need a way to practice the principles we talk about, to connect what they know to the way they really live, and a private space to probe where they're getting stuck, and why.

We can't offer personalized coaching to all of our readers, but we want to bring you the closest thing to it: a book that invites you to explore the parenting philosophies, practices, challenges, and solutions that are particular to your family—all with the goal of raising self-driven children who are capable of running their own lives successfully before they leave home. We want to stop talking *to* you and start talking *with* you. And the best way to take a principle from theoretical to practical is to try it out.

In this introduction, we go over seven principles for raising self-driven kids. Each subsequent chapter focuses on one of the principles, offering you exercises and tools to make these principles your own, to help you fit them into your unique life circumstances with your individual kids and their needs. It encourages you to explore the pressures or obstacles that get in the way of being the parent you want to be so that you can understand those obstacles better and push through them. We'll challenge you to think about what truly matters to you— so that you raise your child based on what you value rather than what you fear.

The last chapter focuses on schools and is written for both parents and educators. We have spoken at hundreds of schools across the country where faculty and administrators are overwhelmed by the troubled emotions and the lack of healthy motivation they observe in their students—and are looking for help. We are glad they are, as we believe that school is often the main source of stress (and thus suffering) in kids' lives—and that schools have tremendous potential to help students thrive by facilitating their sense of autonomy and control. Many of the schools we've worked with are seeking support to make small changes to give students more control. At other schools, administrators want to make encouraging student autonomy a central focus of their educational mission. We want to help schools at any level of interest and commitment to use their power to make school a source of growth and happiness.

The last chapter also addresses the importance of supporting autonomy in teachers. We're in the midst of a countrywide shortage of teachers due largely to the fact that most teachers leave the profession in five years or less—which was true even before the pandemic. We offer suggestions for supporting everyone in the school community to feel and do better by increasing their sense of control over their professional and personal lives.

Whether you are a parent or a teacher, or both, applying the principles we discuss throughout this book will help ease conflict and promote bonding with kids. Building close connections is one of the most important parts of an adult's role with young people. Playing the role of mentor and guide—rather than just imparter of knowledge and manager of behavior—makes our interactions with kids much more effective and satisfying. Moreover, using strategies to help kids find their own motivation can produce much better results than the time-honored carrots and sticks.

Our hope is that this book will bolster your confidence as you maneuver through the various stages and crises of your children's growth, and that it will reassure you that it's right and safe to trust them, to back off, to "get off the crazy train," and to support them in learning to run their own lives.

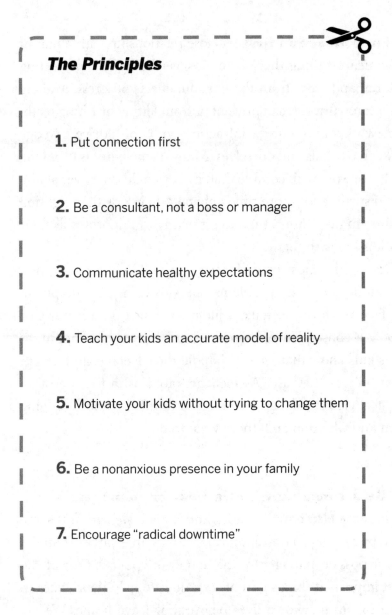

The Principles

1. Put connection first

2. Be a consultant, not a boss or manager

3. Communicate healthy expectations

4. Teach your kids an accurate model of reality

5. Motivate your kids without trying to change them

6. Be a nonanxious presence in your family

7. Encourage "radical downtime"

[Hint: Cut this out and put it on your bedside table or your refrigerator, or use as a bookmark for whatever book you're reading.]

1. Put connection first. A close relationship with a parent is the nearest thing there is to a "silver bullet" for protecting children and teens from the harmful effects of stress. Making this our top priority can prevent us from letting brushing teeth, homework, minor curfew infractions, or chores drive a wedge between our kids and ourselves. Many of the parents of young adults we work with confide that, if they could do it over again, they'd spend a lot more time enjoying their kids than fighting with them over things that aren't nearly as important as their relationship with them.

One of the most powerful ways to build close connection is to understand the problems our kids bring us—or put in our face—before we make a judgment, start on a lecture, or impose a consequence. Expressing empathy is paramount, as it lets kids know that we can handle their feelings and accept them fully as they are. As teenagers told us in focus groups, they feel closest to people who listen to them without judging them and who don't tell them what to do.

2. Be a consultant, not a boss or manager. As kids get into the elementary grades and higher, we can best serve them by playing a consultant role with them—rather than the role of boss or manager (or the homework police). One of the most important things parents can do is to help their children learn to run their own lives before they leave home. We say this because we've worked with so many kids who struggled when they started college or entered the world of work because they did not have adequate experience making decisions, scheduling their time, clarifying their priorities, managing their use of technology, getting themselves into and out of bed on time, asking for help when they need it, and solving their own problems.

A crucial skill that kids need to master in order to run their own lives—and to develop a healthy sense of control—is the ability to make good decisions, and to learn from decisions they later come to think were unwise. And the way kids learn to master this skill is to practice, guided by the advice and wisdom of parents and/or other people who are more experienced. A parent-consultant also lets kids solve their own problems (with support as necessary) as much as possible, because it's by solving their own problems that kids develop high-stress tolerance, emotional resilience, and confidence in their ability to handle difficult situations.

3. **Communicate healthy expectations.** Many kids suffer from what they perceive to be the pressure caused by extremely high parental expectations. Excessive pressure to excel is now believed to be the fourth-leading cause of adolescent unwellness, behind only poverty, trauma, and discrimination. We can communicate expectations for our children that are high *and* healthy by showing confidence in their ability to perform well, which is much more effective than giving them the message that we insist that they do well and that we will be disappointed or angry if they don't.

4. **Teach your kids an accurate model of reality.** Parents are often inclined to see the path to a good life as a narrow road, with steep drop-offs on either side. The right elementary school leads to the right high school leads to the right college leads to the right life. Or the right travel soccer team leads to the right coaches leads to the right college scholarship leads to the right life. In reality, humans find their way to happy adult lives in a myriad of ways. Prestigious colleges do not guarantee happiness—and, in fact, many young people who do attend such institutions are strikingly unhappy and remain so, and plenty of people who have esteemed careers got their start in community college. Further, a poor report card does not lead to a subpar life. Accomplishment is just one factor that contributes to true happiness, which is more closely related to less tangible elements like healthy relationships and a sense of purpose. It's time to change the way we talk to our kids about success and happiness so that they're not terrified of falling off a steep, narrow road.

5. **Motivate your kids without trying to change them.** When kids aren't doing well, parents usually ask how to get them to be more motivated, better behaved, more confident, and/or less anxious. But it turns out that when we try to change others who are not asking us to help them change, we always get resistance and conflict. This is, in part, because almost everyone, including your kid, is often ambivalent about making changes in their lives, including changes that are in their own best interest. So, when our kids are struggling, much of our focus should be on helping them find their own reasons for changing.

6. **Be a nonanxious presence in your family.** Every experienced parent knows that it's much easier to soothe an infant, to help a distressed young child, or to reach an angry teenager if we can stay calm—and don't get stressed and angry ourselves. By developing our ability to stay calm, we can communicate optimism to kids (which is a gift that keeps on giving throughout a lifetime) and teach them to face problems courageously—rather than fearfully. In fact, one of the best ways to help our children avoid high levels of anxiety is to manage our own anxiety effectively. Make home a calm "safe base" where everyone in the family can relax and recover from the stress of daily life. Our nonanxious energy also allows our kids to feel they can bring their problems to us, and that we can handle adversity; it makes it much easier for us to support their autonomy.

7. Encourage "radical downtime" (for your child and yourself). Long before we started working on our books, we often lectured about how technology inevitably makes life more stressful for kids and for adults because it increases the pace of life and, by making things easier to do, creates more work. (Think of how easy it is to send an email and how hard it is to keep your inbox from overflowing.) We explained that, as life goes faster and faster and becomes increasingly demanding, kids and adults need more downtime to offset the mind-racing, mind-scattering, and often mind-numbing effects of technology. This means more "radical" forms of downtime than the time-honored ones (like gardening, playing cards, listening to music) and the new ones (binge-watching Netflix series, watching funny videos, scrolling social media, and playing video games).

For us, "radical downtime" means activities in which you appear to be doing nothing but are actually doing something that is extremely beneficial for your well-being: sleep, mind wandering or daydreaming, and meditation. Sleep is crucial for a developing brain (and for maintaining a developed one!). But that's just one part of the story. "Doing nothing" while awake is also highly beneficial for children's development. Research has shown that periods of mind wandering or day-dreaming foster creativity and problem-solving in children, teens, and adults. Those periods are also crucial for young people's development of empathy and sense of identity, which requires time to reflect on themselves, their experiences, their values, and their relationships. The upshot is: Don't schedule every moment of a kid's day, or of yours. (And, yes, this section covers what to do about the screen time that so often intrudes on quiet!) Finally, meditation is also an important form of radical downtime, as deeply quieting the mind and relaxing the body while wide awake appears to be good for virtually everything.

Everyone Needs a Calm Button . . . and Practice

Recently, Ned had an epic parenting fail with his college-aged daughter, Katie. We'll spare you the details, but what it came down to was that Ned was worried about Katie's happiness, and that worry showed up as trying to solve a problem *for* her. She called him on it. He apologized and sheepishly said, "You know, I should write this down somewhere. Oh, wait, I did! Twice!"

We all need reminders that it's safe to trust our kids, and we need practice doing so. As such, this isn't meant to be a book that you study, but one that you engage with. We're going to ask you lots of questions, and you can answer them in a notebook, directly on the pages of this book, on your phone, through conversation with a friend, your partner, your child, or just in your head. It's not meant to be work, but a means of helping you feel confident that, with practice and reinforcement, you can raise your child to be a self-driven child.

It's also our goal to bring your attention back, again and again, to your values. So often we behave in ways that are reactive or habitual, without asking: What's most important to me when it comes to my relationship with my child? What am I actually trying to achieve? What is my end goal? What really matters? This emphasis on values may be why many parents have told us that these principles greatly helped them with their kids—but also with their relationships with their spouses, partners, parents, siblings, friends, and coworkers.

You can read the principles in order, but you don't need to. If you're struggling with being a nonanxious presence, by all means, skip directly there! The exercises in this book might also strike you differently from year to year in your child's life, and we encourage you to revisit these pages as a way to monitor your own evolution as a parent. Finally, know that many of the principles have overlapping concepts, which we note with a "Cross-Check" at the end of each section. The importance of being a nonanxious presence, for instance, has relevance in every single section of this book. Prioritizing connection shows up in nearly every principle as well.

Above all, take this book and make it your own. Look at us as *your* consultants, but just as your child's life is their own, so is yours.

For parents, and for educators, our belief is that through reflecting on the scenarios and questions we provide, through prompts and conversations with your children and students, and through journaling, the concepts in this book will become a natural part of your thought process. Our expectation is that less time will pass between when you get that worried, *I'm not doing enough!* feeling, and when you push that feeling aside. The goal is that ultimately you will be impervious to that insecurity altogether, that you will know without needing to be reminded that it is indeed safe to trust your child and to give your students more control over their own lives, including their education. And our hope is that the positive feedback loop that comes from this trust will get stronger every day and with every interaction with the young people in your life.

Now let's create that loop.

Put Connection First

Fostering a close connection with your kids is the first of all the principles for a reason: It's foundational. A close parent-child bond is a strong predictor of a child's emotional health and resilience. In fact, one recent longitudinal study found that healthy family relationships offer more protection against a child showing symptoms of depression than neighborhood safety or economic stability. And, even as parents everywhere are rightly concerned about the link between kids' mental health and social media use, it turns out that a strong parent-child relationship mitigates the emotional harm caused by social media.

You can't force a close relationship with kids, and some kids are easier to get close to than others. But we have found that the simple intention of really getting to know your kids as their own individual selves, to let them know that you want to understand their feelings and treat them respectfully, will go a long way in helping you remember your top parenting priority. If you do nothing else with this book, use the five tools we lay out in this chapter, and see your connection with the young people in your life solidify.

But before we delve too deeply into your unique relationship with your child, we first want you to

A healthy bond with your child is the most significant predictor of their emotional health and resilience. Your connection with them is foundational.

reflect on *other* relationships in your life through a series of questions:

Reflection questions:

1. Whom do you feel closest to in your life?

_____

_____

_____

2. What makes you feel close to them?

_____

_____

_____

3. What does this closeness mean to you?

_____

_____

_____

4. Who are the people you know who feel close to you—and what is it about you that makes them feel that way?

_____

_____

_____

5. When you think of other people in your life whom you're not able to be close with, why do you think that is? What is it about the relationship that prevents a strong connection?

_____

_____

_____

6. When you're upset and confide in someone, what sorts of responses make you want to confide in them again? What sorts of responses make you *not* want to?

_____

_____

_____

7. Did you feel close to your own parents?

_____

_____

_____

8. How did they respond when you misbehaved or screwed up?

_____

_____

_____

9. Think about your relationship with the children in your life. And then ask what we think of as the Golden Rule of Parenting: Do you respond to your kids the way you would have liked your parents to respond to you?

_____

_____

_____

10. Do you feel closer to one of your children than to another?

_____

_____

_____

11. Do you think one feels closer to you than another?

_____

_____

_____

We can't answer these questions for you, but there are some commonalities we've noticed in how people answer—and this goes for kids too. As we mentioned in the Introduction, when we ask middle and high schoolers whom they feel closest to and why, they overwhelmingly answer that they feel closest to people who listen to them without judgment and who, while happy to share their opinions when asked, don't always tell them what to do. They describe people who take them as they are, treat them respectfully, apologize when they screw up, and give them space to solve their own problems. While sometimes this person is a parent, it's often a friend or a teacher, or another adult who isn't directly responsible for their well-being.

It makes sense that the parent-child connection is often fraught. Parents aren't just there to hang out. They have a *job* to do: raising a decent and functional human being to adulthood safely. They have a *stake* in a way that the cool journalism teacher doesn't. Parents are the ones worrying about grades, making sure kids put on deodorant and clean their rooms, and fretting about safety while also, by the way, likely holding down their own jobs and trying to keep a household running and maybe raising other kids too. They don't always have the luxury of chatting, free of an agenda. And anyway, aren't they supposed to be a *parent*, not a friend?

All of these things are true.

And yet.

See above about the research on parent-child connection.

Then, put that conclusion together with what a close connection to someone means to *you*, and how you achieve it.

Which leaves us to the task at hand: How do you foster connection even while you're doing all the important things like keeping your kid alive and relatively high-functioning? There is no one-size-fits-all method that works for everyone every time. However, the expression of empathy is often the most powerful, and acts as the soil in which the relationship can grow. This chapter will give you five go-to tools; happily, it starts with an assignment about joy.

> When asked why they feel closest to certain people, adolescents overwhelming have the same answer: "Because they listen to me without judging me and don't always tell me what to do."

1. Find opportunities for fun

We've often said that the most important thing parents can do for their kids is to enjoy being with them, which helps kids see themselves as joy-producing—rather than frustration-, anxiety-, or anger-producing—organisms. And the best part of this is that it means making room for things that are *fun*, because having fun with your kid is one of the surefire ways to connect with them. In a world full of must-dos, fun often gets short shrift.

Think of how many hours—or minutes—this past week were spent on having fun with your kids.

▶ What were you doing?

_____

▶ Why was it fun?

_____

▶ Was it fun for all of you?

_____

Joy doesn't have to be expensive or involve inordinate planning. One night as Ned's family was finishing dinner, his teenagers asked if they could bring out their phones and show Ned and Vanessa (their mom) a funny TikTok. Ned and Vanessa agreed, and one TikTok turned into twenty (as these things do), each one funnier than the last. It was so enjoyable that they decided to make it a regular Tuesday-night ritual.

When Bill's children were younger (years before TikTok), Friday night was movie night. The family spent hours watching movies they all enjoyed, and everyone looked forward to movie night each week. By the time the kids were teenagers they still often wanted to hang out and watch movies as a family on Fridays. And when Bill or Starr (their mom) would pick out a dud, they'd be playfully teased about it for years to come—and still are!

▶ What are five enjoyable activities you can share with your kids?

_____

_____

_____

_____

_____

▶ What gets in the way of "fun time"?

_____

_____

_____

_____

_____

▶ How can you remove those obstacles?

_____

_____

_____

_____

▶ How can you reserve time for joy next week? And the next?

_____

_____

_____

_____

Bonus points: Individual time. We are big proponents of one-on-one time as a way to facilitate closeness. We're not saying it's easy, but it's incredibly effective. Try this experiment: For a whole month, spend time (ideally an hour but do the best you can) every week one-on-one with each of your kids. This is naturally easier for someone with two kids than with five! Let them determine how you spend this hour, within reason. After a month, reflect on what those hours did for your relationship. Can you keep this practice up? If not an hour, how long? If not every week, how often? Mark the next private-time session on your calendar as the current one ends.

Commit to staying off your phones during this time, unless you've decided to spend the hour together on a phone-related activity. Several studies have been done on the effects on kids' emotional development of parental "phubbing," a term coined by language experts to describe snubbing someone by looking at your phone instead of paying attention to them. Not surprisingly, research has shown that phubbing is increasingly prevalent in families, is related to poor parent-child relationships, appears to have a negative effect on young children's emotional development, and is associated with depressive symptoms and cell phone addiction in adolescents.

FAQ: But wait—what if my kid doesn't want to spend time with me?

Most kids go through phases, particularly during adolescence, in which they really don't want to hang out with their parents. In these instances, you can take a chore and make it into connection time. If they're learning to drive, your time with them can be a driving lesson. It might not be enjoyable (or relaxing!) for you, necessarily, but it's still time together. Or perhaps you skip the car pool this week and drive them to their hockey practice yourself, using the car time as catch-up time. Or do something you both enjoy but don't usually do together, like getting a drink at Starbucks. Or perhaps there's an errand they've really needed to run, and you offer to drive them to do it. You can always suggest lunch on the way, or even just enjoy listening to music together en route. Even going to their games, watching their dance or gymnastics practices, watching them play video games for a few minutes (or playing with them), watching television together, schlepping them to

We really get to know someone when we spend time alone with them.

rehearsals or practices, or listening to them practice an instrument gives kids the message that you care about them and want to spend time with them, even if you aren't interacting a ton.

2. Investigate and facilitate the right time, place, and body language for emotional openness

All kids are different. Increasing connection with *your* child is a bit of an investigatory process.

First, begin to note the circumstances in which your kid tends to open up to you.

- ▶ Is it when he is physically moving, like walking somewhere with you?

- ▶ Is it right after school or work?

- ▶ Right before she goes to bed?

- ▶ At breakfast?

- ▶ In the car at night, like when driving home from a practice or school event?

- ▶ When was the last time you felt a close connection with them? Where were you and why do you think it happened then?

Next, once you've identified your child's window of openness, be there. It might not be at the most convenient time for you, but the opening is an opportunity you want to seize if you possibly can. One mother told us she could tell something was bothering her daughter when she picked her up from school.

The daughter didn't want to talk about it on the way home. The mom tried again after dinner, and the daughter was still very closed off. So the mom went into her daughter's room right before lights out and just lay down on the bed and waited. Third time was the charm, and the daughter opened up about something really upsetting that someone had said to her at school that day. In fact, bedtime is often the most likely time for kids to open up, as they're done with the tasks of their day, their defenses are down, and they can't push off uncomfortable feelings anymore.

Third, pay attention to the body language your kid responds to. When children are small, best communication practices maintain that you should get on their level, look them in the eye, and have an open posture and a gentle voice. But things change. For older kids and adolescents, sometimes that kind of focus is too much. Is your kid most open in the car, when he doesn't have to make eye contact with you? Is it when you're watching a show or a game together? Or when someone else is present? While all kids will be different here—and some will indeed need to be sitting on the same level as you, eye contact and all—what's true across the board is that you shouldn't be looking at your phone.

If your child needs your attention but you're just too busy right now, say something like, "What you're saying is really important to me, and I want to give it my full attention. I can't do that until I finish working / making dinner / etc., so let's find a time after I've finished to talk about it. How about after dinner tonight?"

If your kid doesn't initiate or is reluctant to open up, try sharing your own feelings and being a little vulnerable. Tell them about an embarrassing situation at work, for example, or about a conflict with a coworker or a problem you were trying to solve. When Bill used to teach preschool, he discovered that when kids were reluctant to talk, the best way to help them open up was to talk about his own experiences or his favorite things. He's found that it works for older kids too.

3. Put connection before judgment, even when it's hard

It's easy enough to connect with your kids while watching funny TikToks, but what about when they're upset? Or angry at you? Or expressing something you strongly disagree with?

Imagine this scenario: Your middle school daughter is full of angst one evening because she knows she bombed a math test. "It was so unfair!" she exclaims. "Mr. Christensen put all this stuff on the test that he didn't even cover in class. It feels like he's just out to get us. This always happens to me. I always get the meanest teachers."

There are multiple ways to respond here:

A. Reassure her that she should be able to retake the test, that Mr. Christensen tends to be generous about retakes.

B. Tell her that you understand. You can imagine how upsetting it would be to see things on a test that you didn't realize were going to be on there.

C. Tell her you had the same thing happen to you in geometry, but you muddled through, and look where you are today. Also, she's doing great in English, so yay!

D. Pressure test some of her assumptions. Did Mr. Christensen assign an exercise about the material, even if he didn't explicitly go over it in class? Surely she can't really think that Mr. Christensen gets his kicks by seeing kids fail? Remind her he's a decent guy and that she's liked him at other points in the year.

E. Ask, "Is there a way I can help?" but don't push your involvement further if she says no.

Which of these responses resonates the most with you, and how you've handled similar situations in the past? How would your kid respond to each?

_____

_____

_____

_____

_____

_____

_____

_____

_____

Option A is perhaps the most instinctual for parents. As mammals, we're wired to protect and soothe our young. We have what is called a "righting reflex," meaning that when our kids are uncomfortable, we want to make things right by solving their problems for them, usually logically. And it's very logical that there is a "fix" to the situation. But when people are upset, whether they're age four or ninety-four, logic isn't all that helpful. It's also true that, as we'll emphasize in the next chapter, we want to let kids solve their own problems whenever possible.

Option B is a good start. It validates her feelings and allows her to blow off some frustration. But the problem is, she often frames her life this way—that she is the victim and the world is out to get her, and you worry about that. Shouldn't you be able to point out her faulty thinking? Isn't this in fact the *role* of a parent?

Option C is intended to show you understand, and that you've been there, and to lower the heat a bit. The tricky thing about this response is that it moves the focus from her to you. Kids are masters at detecting evasion. (Remember how when she was three, you could distract her from wanting a cookie by offering her a toy? If only!) It also risks leaving her feeling unheard.

Option D feels honest to you, and reflects the nuanced thinking you want her to adopt. You also think, *If I don't push her on this, who will?* But it may cause her to feel criticized and invalidated—meaning that we think her feelings are "wrong"—and is likely to put her on the defensive. It also risks that she will shut down and choose not to confide in you in the future. She may later realize that she overreacted or misread the situation, but our goal is to help her come to the realization herself. If we want our children to understand and trust their feelings, it's important that they feel understood and accepted.

Option E indicates you are there to offer support, but it's her problem to figure out how to fix. It could leave her stuck in

Logic doesn't calm emotions—empathy and validation do.

the same morass of hard feelings if she doesn't yet know what to do.

So, if all of these answers have problems, what's the right thing to do? Importantly, none of these are wrong. Still, we like starting with **Option B** because it focuses on empathy first, and then bringing in a little of **Option D** and **E**.

Once you have listened to your daughter's frustrations, let her know that you're trying to understand ("If I have this right, you feel that the test was really unfair"), and validate the emotional place she's coming from ("If I had a teacher who tested me on stuff I hadn't been taught, I'd be upset too"). Chances are that she'll calm down. Once she feels "heard," she may even say something like, "I think that maybe I should have studied more." If you then employ **Option E** ("Is there a way I can help?"), you're signaling your willingness to be part of the problem-solving process if your child wants you to—without trying to shove a solution down her throat.

This is where parts of **Option D** come in. When you suspect she's ready, you can ask her if she wants your take on the whole situation. You want to give her feedback, but in a way that preserves the relationship and her willingness to share things with you. If she says yes, you can offer a different framing to consider. At that point, you can tell her how *you* see it (i.e., that Mr. Christensen probably isn't an evil schemer out to get her and her classmates!). And if she doesn't want to hear your take? Leave it alone for the time being.

If, however, she gets stuck in a loop of feeling sorry for herself, you don't have to stay at the pity party all night. Imagine that hours have passed and she is clearly wallowing in her feelings of self-righteous

> Good parenting doesn't mean agreeing with or approving of everything your kid says.

victimization and wants you to be the "Witness to Her Pain." At that point, listening and empathizing is no longer productive, and you can say, "I know this is really hard for you, but I don't think that talking about it more right now is going to help you. Can you think of anything you could do to make yourself feel better?"

You may not have encountered this particular scenario. But chances are excellent there are a plethora of situations you encounter weekly in which your child's take on something is wildly different from what you believe. Do any of these sound familiar?

▶ "This new girl, Tara, joined my group at lunch today, and she's going to ruin everything! She's just not like us!"

▶ "I hate that we have to go to Grandma's every Sunday night. It's not fair!"

▶ "I can't stand [insert any stereotype here] kids. They are all so annoying."

▶ "It was so unfair of Ms. Karten to dress-code me! These dress code rules are so ridiculous."

▶ "I suck at math."

▶ "Everybody in my science class understands the stuff better than me."

▶ "Mr. Johnson is *always* criticizing me for the littlest things."

▶ "But everyone in seventh grade has a cell phone!"

In these situations, what gets in the way of choosing the response you most want to have? Is it feeling frazzled, interrupted, or frustrated? Do you get a surge of fear as you connect this response with others like it and detect a pattern ("my child has a victim mentality / has low self-esteem / is entitled / is becoming mean")? Is it that you feel compelled to fix the problem? What triggers make you take the bait and choose self-righteousness or moralizing over connection?

_____

_____

_____

_____

_____

_____

_____

_____

Reflection questions:

▶ What scenarios repeatedly come up with your kid?

_____

_____

_____

▶ What, if anything, makes it hard for you just to listen?

_____

_____

_____

4. Use the SURE checklist

In our book *What Do You Say?*, we shared an acronym to help parents navigate conversations with their kids in ways that prioritize connection. Here we offer it as a checklist.

❏ **Stay calm**. If you are frustrated or agitated going into a conversation, it's not the time to have it! For more on this, see Principle 6.

❏ **Understand before judging.** Be careful not to assume you have a solid grasp of a situation. Often there are layers and layers behind a kid's upset, and it takes some time and curiosity to get to the bottom of it. Ask questions intended to help you gain understanding.

❏ **Reflect back.** So often we just want to be *heard* when we're upset. Paraphrase your child's account of events, and say things like, in the bombed-math-test scenario, "What I understand you're saying is that you feel that the test was really unfair." Reflective listening isn't intuitive to most people—it's a learned skill—but it's so powerful that it's been a central tool in many kinds of therapy for sixty-five years.

❏ **Explore options**. Problem-solving absolutely has a role in fostering connection with your kid. You just want to do it *last*, after they have felt seen and supported in whatever is going on with them. And you want to remind yourself that every problem has more than one solution. Your kid's preferred solution might not be the solution you think is best—and that's okay! Ask them if they'd like to explore some solutions together. There's much more on skills for doing so in the next chapter.

And while you might jot the checklist down now, or mentally run through the SURE acronym during your next complicated conversation, you won't always have to. As with anything, the more you practice SURE, the more second nature its steps become. Fighter pilots are taught a formula for helping them make quick decisions under pressure. (It's called the OODA loop, and it stands for Observe, Orient, Decide, Act.) Pilots practice implementing this loop hundreds of times before they are sent on a mission so that it becomes so automatic that they can remember and implement it even when under extreme pressure.

While we're usually not using the SURE formula in life-threatening situations, the more practice you have with it, the easier it will be to use it when your child is in a stressful situation and needs your help.

Trap Alert!

Think of your past communications with your child that did not go well, and see if any of these common traps came into play.

▶ **Imbalance of tasking vs. connecting.** There are plenty of to-dos that we need to mark off each day in a busy life, and that our kid does too. But it's easy to fall into a trap where it's *all* we talk about with our kids. "Have you done your homework?" "Can you clean the kitchen?" "Did you write back to your chem teacher yet?" "Don't forget to send that thank-you note! Have you done it yet?" Are you tasking them more than you're talking to them, agenda-free? If so, they'll be practiced at tuning you out completely. In a study of hunter-gatherers in Central Africa, anthropologist Sheina Lew-Levy found that an adult verbally instructed a child only three times per hour. Journalist Michaeleen Doucleff cites the study in her book *Hunt, Gather, Parent*, and noted that when she tracked her own commands for fifteen minutes, she was on pace for sixty times an hour!

▶ **Defaulting to the "righting reflex."** As we mentioned, as a parent you are wired to want to make everything right in your child's world (and, in yours!) through the use of logical problem-solving or advice based on your experience. Recognize this impulse, but don't give into it. You don't have to fix everything. You want to soothe and make everything okay, but sometimes you can't and you shouldn't. If you deprive your child of opportunities to solve their own problems, it weakens them because their brain does not get the experience it needs to go into coping mode (rather than avoidance or freaking-out mode) when stressed. (More on this in Principle 3.)

▶ **Assuming that to connect, you have to be less like a parent and more like a friend.** That's not so! You can have a close connection with your kid *and still:*

  ▶ disagree with them

  ▶ insist they clean their room and do their own laundry

  ▶ tell them they can't go to the concert in another city that ends at two a.m. on a school night. (Unless it's Taylor Swift. If they scored tickets, well, you've got to make it happen for them!)

  ▶ not let them drive if they didn't sleep for at least eight hours the two previous nights

▸ require them to pay at least part of an important purchase they want to make

Our kids still connect with us when we set limits in a respectful way, with input from them where possible. In fact, although they won't necessarily say it, they want limits because boundaries make children feel safe.

▸ **Turning everything into a teaching moment.** We've both been guilty of this—honestly, most parents have. But if you take your child's decision to confide in you, and seize the opportunity only to drop some knowledge or wisdom about whatever the issue is, you've lost the opportunity to connect. Elizabeth, a high school sophomore, complained to her dad one morning that she hated the probability unit they were working on in math. Her dad—eager to foster intellectual curiosity in his daughter—started talking to her about all of the ways probability shows up in her life, such as, "Let's suppose we try to get playoff tickets when they first go on sale. What's the probability that we will?" She stared at him a moment, then asked, "Let's suppose that a dad spends his daughter's last years in high school talking about probability. What do you think the probability is that she will call him when she's in college?" Touché.

▸ **Jealousy of another adult or parent.** Naturally you want your kid to talk to *you* when they have something important to share. And sometimes, they'll go to someone else, whether it's another parent, an aunt or uncle, a teacher or coach, or even a friend's parent. Not every parent has to be everything all the time. Families are living, breathing systems. When Bill's kids were growing up, sometimes they would be closer to him, and other times they'd be closer to their mother. What's important is that they were talking to a trusted person over the age of sixteen!

5. Bring it back to values

It's easy in parenting to get so caught up in the emotion of the moment—or the sheer busyness of life—that we lose sight of the goals we're aiming for. If you're finding an interaction with your child challenging, or you're not sure what to say or do in a given situation, bring it back to your big-picture values. What are you trying to do with the interaction? Is there a particular outcome you want? Do you want to solve the problem? Maintain a close connection? What are you trying to do long-term?

Okay, it's kind of a trick question. The answer to that last question should always be "Maintain a close connection." Let connection guide you, always and always.

Changing the Energy

INSTEAD OF THIS	TRY THIS
I've told you a million times!	Let me know how I can support you.
That doesn't sound so bad.	That sucks.
Did you do your homework today?	Do you want me to check in with you about school-work? If so, when would be a good time?
I can't believe she did that to you!	It must be hard to feel that your friend betrayed you.

 **Cross-Check:**

Principle 6—*Be a Nonanxious Presence in Your Family*

Principle 2—*Be a Consultant, Not a Boss or Manager*

Be a Consultant, Not a Boss or Manager

In early November a couple of years ago, we personally knew seven kids who had started college at the end of the summer and were already back home, living with their parents. In each case, the kids' failure to make it in college on their first try wasn't because they weren't smart or academically competent enough. It was because they were unable to manage the demands of living and going to school independently. During the few weeks they'd been in college, their sleep cycles became dysregulated, they missed morning classes, they played video games way too much, they avoided talking to their professors when they didn't understand the material being taught or needed an extension on an assignment, and they fell far behind in their studying because they couldn't resist the multiple temptations offered by college life. Many also stopped taking their medications. In each case, these kids had reckoned with similar challenges in their senior year of high school. November might be a bit early to call it quits, but plenty of their classmates would soon catch up; roughly thirty percent of freshmen don't return for their sophomore year.

As all parents know, we have to let go eventually, and we don't want to do it all at once. That's not fair to our kids, and doesn't set them up for success. The way we see it, one of the most important goals as parents is to help our kids become skilled at running their own lives while they're home—so they don't run aground when they leave. We want to give them practice making decisions, learning from bad ones, and exercising their own judgment, which is how kids learn to trust themselves, and we want them to be practiced at taking care of their bodies, managing their time, solving their problems, and reaching out when they need to before they're on their own. And so it's useful for us to act like *consultants* to our kids, rather than their bosses or managers. We want to be the party who asks "What are you hoping to accomplish?" and "What do you need help with?" and who offers support and guidance, but not mandates, so that by the time our kids leave home, they're ready.

Not only does the consultant approach make the most sense for practical reasons, but it makes the most sense for scientific ones. When kids make hard decisions and solve their own problems, they activate their prefrontal cortex, which dampens their stress response, allowing them to think clearly and to find solutions to their problems. Over time, these experiences wire their brains in a way that facilitates their learning to trust their own decisions and to go into "coping mode" when they're stressed, rather than panicking or avoiding hard situations altogether. The neurons that fire for decision-making get stronger as they're used. Asking an eighteen-year-old to make decisions about housing, classes, and finances—let alone drinking, sleeping, and partying—when they haven't had a chance to develop these brain capabilities is like asking someone who has rarely gotten off the couch in their life to run a 10k race, and to run it fast. And, because tapping into our emotions is extremely important for making good decisions, kids need a lot of practice considering their own feelings (and the feelings of others) as they are making decisions.

The Role of a Parent Consultant

Effective parent consultants do three main things:

1. Offer their help and advice but don't force it.

2. Support kids in making their own decisions (with input from more experienced people) and go with kids' decisions unless most reasonable people would deem them crazy, unsafe, or both.

3. Encourage kids to solve their own problems.

Exercise: Raising a Competent Young Adult

Regardless of whether your kids are elementary schoolers or high schoolers, take a few minutes to think about them at the age of eighteen or nineteen. Imagine they have graduated from high school and are venturing out into the world in some way. You're still around for support, of course, but not in the same way. Little by little, over the years you've extracted yourself from the daily running of their life. Maybe your child is going away to live in a dorm at the college they'll be attending. Or maybe they're attending vocational school or taking some time away from school to practice adulting and to find out more about what they want in life. Or maybe they're sticking close to home and working a job. Regardless of their particular path, when you think about this young adult, what are the central life skills you want them to have? What are the practical tasks you want them to know how to do?

Write them here but feel free to use additional paper if you need to. We've started you out with some suggestions, but feel free to add.

CATEGORY	SKILLS	
Health and hygiene	Getting to bed early enough to be well rested	_____
	Getting out of bed on their own	_____
	Preparing basic meals	_____
	Showering regularly	_____
	Doing laundry	_____
	Clipping nails	_____
	Taking medication regularly	_____
	Calling for doctor appointments when needed	_____
	Seeking help for mental health needs	_____
	Moderating (or avoiding) drinking and drug use	_____
	Using healthy coping mechanisms	_____
Transportation	Figuring out public transportation	_____
	Driving competently	_____
	Doing basic car maintenance	_____
	Booking a train or flight	_____
	Navigating an airport, train station, or subway station	_____
	Calling an Uber or taxi	_____
Post–secondary education and/or training	Keeping up with course load	_____
	Tracking and completing assignments on time	_____
	Studying adequately for tests	_____
	Seeking tutorial support if needed	_____
	Advocating for necessary accommodations	_____
	Moderating the use of electronic entertainment, including television, social media, and video games	_____

CATEGORY	SKILLS	
Work	Researching and applying for jobs	_____
	Creating a résumé	_____
	Interviewing successfully	_____
	Calling out harassment	_____
	Setting boundaries	_____
	Managing time effectively	_____
	Planning	_____
	Meeting deadlines	_____
	Being punctual	_____
	Negotiating for fair pay	_____
Financial	Paying bills on time	_____
	Understanding credit cards and how they work	_____
	Doing taxes if necessary	_____
	Creating a budget and sticking to it	_____
	Saving	_____
Interpersonal	Asking for help	_____
	Apologizing when they've hurt someone	_____
	Voicing dissent	_____
	Being an ally	_____
	Resisting pressure	_____
	Managing in a crisis	_____
	Setting boundaries	_____
	Practicing safe sex	_____
	Compromising	_____
	Initiating getting together	_____
	Making new friends	_____
Home/habitat management	Shopping for groceries	_____
	Cooking a healthy meal	_____
	Being prepared for emergencies	_____
	Understanding a lease	_____

Keep this list, and keep adding to it as you think of important milestones and mundane tasks alike.

Now, we want to redo the table from above but with a different spin. Write down how *you* learned these skills. Did someone teach them to you (parents, teacher, books, TV) or did you seek out the knowledge? Do you think you learned these skills in the best way? Also, *when* did you learn these skills? Did you learn them by the time you needed them?

CATEGORY	SKILLS	HOW I LEARNED	HOW I FEEL ABOUT HOW I LEARNED
Health and hygiene			
Transportation			
Post–secondary education and/ or training			
Work			
Financial			

CATEGORY	SKILLS	HOW I LEARNED	HOW I FEEL ABOUT HOW I LEARNED
Interpersonal			
Home/habitat management			

Reflection questions:

- When you left home, did you feel you were ready? Did you feel capable of running your own life? Making your own appointments? Taking your medication? Doing your own laundry? Making basic meals? Were you able to get yourself into and out of bed on time? Had you held a part-time or full-time job? If you're young enough to have grown up online, could you set limits on how much time you spent online? Could you manage your academic responsibilities independently?

_____

_____

_____

_____

_____

_____

- What, if anything, do you wish your parents had done differently when it came to preparing you for a life of independence? Did they help you develop healthy ways of pursuing your success? If you learned skills later than you wished, did it have anything to do with what your parents did or didn't do?

_____

_____

_____

_____

_____

_____

_____

- How have the ways you've learned to be an adult impacted the ways you're teaching your child? In an age where most basic things can be looked up on YouTube, how is your role different from that of your parents'?

_____

_____

_____

_____

_____

_____

_____

Exercise: Empowering Young People

Over the next week, pay attention to the way tasks are handed out in your family, and what you do for others that, if pressed, you might not need to. Are there things your child is asking you to hand over to them? (Granted, they are probably not begging to do their laundry, but perhaps they want to handle their own car-pool plans, or meal planning.) Then, fill in the chart below.

WHAT DO YOU TAKE RESPONSIBILITY FOR THAT YOUR CHILD COULD PROBABLY DO?	WHAT DOES YOUR CHILD WANT TO BE RESPONSIBLE FOR THAT THEY'RE CURRENTLY NOT?

Remember, *your ultimate objective as a parent is to raise a young adult who is capable of managing their own life.* At a lecture we gave just before the pandemic to 150 high school counselors from across the country, we asked them if it's fair to say that, if a student isn't running the college search and admission process himself, he's not ready to go to college. One attendee stood up and said, "Absolutely. I tell parents that all the time." When we asked the audience to raise their hands if they agreed, every hand went up. In a later discussion with a smaller group of counselors, they explained that if a kid isn't identifying appropriate schools, keeping track of requirements and deadlines, and completing applications and letters without his parents' constant reminders, the likelihood of his succeeding in college the following year is virtually zero.

> One of the best messages you can give a teenager: "I have confidence in your ability to make decisions about your own life and to learn from your mistakes."

Parents and kids don't seem to heed this message, as they see getting into college as the finish line of a race. But getting into college these days isn't hard. (Really! More on this in Principle 4!) Managing the academic, social, and self-management demands of college is much harder, and kids should show that they're ready to handle those responsibilities before we send them off.

One of the trickiest parts about parenting is that you constantly have to step back—not just in a child's junior or senior year of high school, but long before. And yet there's no schedule or alarm bell that says, "Ding-ding! Okay, *now!* Now is the time to stop making lunch for them." Instead, we get caught up in routines, habits, and roles. Our kids rely on us to play those roles, and we're usually okay with them too because:

1. it's often easier and more time-efficient,

2. it gives us a sense of control,

3. it's nice to be needed,

4. it's a way of holding on to our kids—even if we only feel this subconsciously, and

5. we want to keep them from failing—and thus suffering.

Adopting the consultant approach isn't intuitive to a lot of parents. They mistake it with being permissive, not setting limits, or just letting their kids have their way. In fact, though, parenting styles don't have to swing so dramatically from authoritarian (the "boss" parent) to permissive (the "do whatever you want!" parent). There is a middle ground, a style known as authoritative parenting, that sets limits as necessary and treats kids respectfully, but also offers a lot of freedom for the child to move around within those limits. On the next page, we've included some scenarios and the typical responses of each parenting style. We've also left some blanks for you to put in scenarios from your life and your child's, and how different parenting styles would apply.

Don't routinely do things for kids that they're capable of doing themselves.

SCENARIO	AUTHORITARIAN	PERMISSIVE	AUTHORITATIVE
A five-year-old doesn't want to wear her coat to the park.	"You don't think you'll be cold, but you will be. So you're wearing it."	"Okay, that's fine!" (Thinking: *We'll just come home and get it if she changes her mind.*)	"Why don't you step outside for a second and make sure you're good with that decision? If so, then you don't need to wear it, but just know that we won't be able to come back for it, so you might be cold."
A ten-year-old doesn't want to study for a spelling test.	"You haven't studied, so no baseball practice tonight."	Doesn't ever ask or engage in conversations about homework.	"I know you want to do well on that test. I trust that you know what you need to do for that to happen, so I'll leave you alone about it. But I will be available from seven to eight if you need any help studying."
A twelve-year-old wants to quit baseball in the middle of the season because he's not playing well.	"Absolutely not. You committed, so you're going to play."	"Okay, you can quit. I know you hate it."	"I know that you're discouraged because you haven't been playing as well this year as you did last year. And I know that it sucks when you don't do well. You committed for the whole season, though, and it's a family value to follow through on our commitments whenever we can. What ideas do you have for how we might make the rest of the season feel better for you?"
A seventeen-year-old applying for college is only looking at the most elite schools and doesn't have any "safety" options.	"You need to apply to five schools you'll definitely get into. Here's a list I came up with."	"I'm sure you'll get in. Anyone who doesn't accept you would be such a fool."	"I'm not going to force you to apply anywhere. But I think it would be a useful exercise to think about what you'll do if you don't get in to any of the schools on your list. Would you like to talk that through?"

Most parents take an authoritarian approach not because they're jerks but because they love their kids more than anything and want them to have every possible advantage in life. Also, they have much more experience and they want their kids to benefit from it. Many parents were raised with an authoritarian approach themselves, and they may worry that they'll be criticized for spoiling their children if they aren't "controlling their kids." But a controlling approach doesn't work long-term, and we'd argue that it doesn't work short-term either. Parents seem to get this when we unpack what it means to *make* a child do something. As we said in the Introduction, you can't, for instance, make your son do his homework. You can tell him a hundred times that he needs to, and you can offer an incentive or create an environment unpleasant enough that he's likely to comply, but if he chooses not to, what can you really do? Prop his eyes open? Hold his fingers to the keyboard? Do it for him? When, technically, is he the one doing it?

That's an extreme example, but stick with us, because it's a good one to illustrate what happens when we try to coerce our kids. There is a distribution of energy that goes into every task, and the more energy a parent, teacher, tutor, coach, or mentor spends trying to get a kid to do something, the less energy the kid will spend. Many kids who don't seem to care about school have a mountain of supports propping them up, moving them through each day. They come to rely on those supports, in part because doing so makes them less anxious in the short run. ("I'll let them worry about it so I don't have to.") However, letting other people take responsibility for something that is really their responsibility limits their sense of agency, and can actually *increase* their anxiety over time by making them less confident in their ability to manage their own lives. Parents need to allow for a sequence of growth:

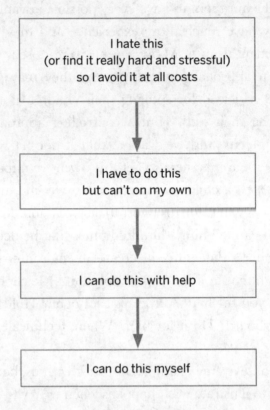

I hate this
(or find it really hard and stressful)
so I avoid it at all costs

I have to do this
but can't on my own

I can do this with help

I can do this myself

What Would You Do? The "EveryParent" Question of Technology

Parents Carla and David found themselves constantly at loggerheads with their thirteen-year-old son, Zack, about screen time. Sound familiar? We'd guess so, as screen time is invariably the very first issue parents want to talk to us about. Although Zack did not have a smartphone, he did have a watch from which he could call and text his friends. Carla and David and Zack worked out limits on screen time: no noneducational screen time during the week, and two hours on Friday, Saturday, and Sunday. Zack agreed that the limits were reasonable, and he also told his parents that he wanted their help monitoring his use.

Time after time, though, Zack found ways to sneak screen time during the week by using his school computer to watch TikTok for hours, or having a friend over so they could use the friend's device. Carla and David felt they constantly had to monitor Zack because, as doctors, they were all too aware that the technology that kids love is designed to be addictive, and they knew Zack struggled with self-discipline. "He doesn't have the executive functioning skills yet to make himself stop," they explained, "and it's not fair to essentially hand a kid an addictive substance and say, 'Here—have at it!,'" which is what they interpreted our "parent-as-consultant" advice to be. They knew from past experience that Zack was much calmer and nicer when he didn't have access to tech.

But they also admitted their approach wasn't working. Whenever Zack was caught sneaking screen time, the agreed-upon consequence was that he would lose the screen time he *did* have for a week. And so the pattern continued, with more tension growing each time, and with Carla and David trusting Zack less and less. When, on occasion, they gave him free rein over his tech usage to see if he would exercise any restraint, he was instead like a pig in mud, on a screen for ten or eleven hours straight.

If you were Carla and David, what would you do?

▶ Would you loosen restrictions for the sake of the relationship?

_____

_____

_____

_____

▶ Would you double down on enforcement? Figure out how to block TikTok and other programs at least until he turns fourteen or fifteen, when his brain is more developed?

_____

_____

_____

_____

▶ Would you give him total power to stop the arguing and see how long it would take him to realize how much is too much?

_____

_____

_____

_____

A few factors came into play in our advice. First, we shared that we didn't think their expectation was entirely reasonable, as we thought that they were holding Zack to too high of a standard. (We watched tons of terrible TV as kids, and, for the most part, we turned out okay.)

"But we agreed on what the times should be," Carla said. "We didn't just pull that out of the air—we were collaborative with him. And he agreed that he doesn't want to be on screens all the time and that he needs us to help him police it."

That may be, but Zack had a really close relationship with his parents. He actually wanted more than anything to please them, and he knew they frowned on screen time. The standards they held for him were high, and thus he was holding himself to standards that were high—too high, clearly, as he wasn't able to follow them.

We also encouraged them to look beyond the studies about teens and tech use that had (understandably!) scared them, to consider *how* Zack was using screens, and why. For all they knew, at school all anyone talked about was the latest trending meme or video, and he was missing out. At his age, that's a big deal. Social media scholar danah boyd frequently emphasizes that teens aren't addicted to screen time as much as they're addicted to each other. Pop culture is currency in their world, and while we don't want to give kids carte blanche to watch whatever content they want, we also don't want to seal them off from that world completely.

What's more, if Carla and David felt that by depriving Zack long enough, he'd stop wanting screens, that was not likely to work. Many kids, in fact, go the other way—catching up in spectacular and dangerous ways when their parents are no longer looking over their shoulder.

As for the times they'd given Zack total freedom and he'd gorged himself, Zack's response makes sense to us. One day (or even a week, or several weeks) of total autonomy isn't going to get screen time out of his system. For one thing, he will know he's on borrowed time; and for another, it takes a lot of time and practice to learn to make good decisions around tech.

We suggested they say something like this to Zack: "We don't want to police you all the time, but we don't want to feel like we're the worst parents in the world by letting you be on screens too much, knowing as we do how addictive this stuff is." The goal was to move in the direction of healthy use, and for that Zack needed more practice regulating himself, but with Carla and David's support. They might suggest starting with *increased* screen time, acknowledging that if he's sneaking it, the time limits they'd previously set probably didn't feel reasonable to Zack. They could also figure out ways Zack could be more in control by doing things like adjusting his settings to cut off his access after a certain point, or deciding on a few hours of the evening that would always be tech-free. And they might brainstorm with Zack about what activities he could shift to when his screen time was over, which could help him make the transition.

"But what about the fact that we know his brain is just not mature enough to stop?" said David. "Isn't giving him so much control unfair to him, in a way?"

We support legislation to limit kids' access to the internet and social media until they're older. Until that happens, however, all kids, including Zack, *need* practice making good decisions more than they deserve it. That's how they develop the muscle.

And we did not suggest that Carla and David step away from Zack's tech usage altogether. They could still find ways to see what he was watching and doing, and keep the conversation about how much was enough ongoing. But Zack might screw up, watch too much TikTok, and fail to do his schoolwork. Okay, then what? They could then have a conversation about what he thinks he should do differently next time. Maybe he'd say something like, "I want to be on screens tonight, but can you take my phone until after I've done my homework?"

Again, the long-term goal is for Zack to be able to regulate technology independently, just as he'll need to learn to regulate eating and sleeping independently. Don't panic that at age thirteen he will never develop his regulation muscle—he just hasn't yet. His prefrontal cortex has a long way to go, and the way to encourage it along is by giving him more—rather than less—autonomy.

Exercise: Changing the Energy Equation

Think of issues where you feel continually at loggerheads with your child. It could be about brushing teeth, sleep, church attendance, screen time, schoolwork, chores, health, organization, or anything else. How much energy are you spending on fixing the issue, and how much energy is your child spending?

ISSUE	PERCENTAGE OF ENERGY YOU AND OTHERS (NOT YOUR CHILD) ARE GIVING	PERCENTAGE OF ENERGY YOUR CHILD IS GIVING
Zack can't manage our boundaries around screen usage.	Ninety percent. His parents, as we police usage, set and enforce consequences, and initiate conversations about usage.	Ten percent. Zack did participate in a collaborative conversation about usage, and tolerates our consequences for sneaking more time.

You are likely thinking, *But I'm the only one who cares about it! My kid doesn't think it's an issue that needs fixing.* That's why it's important, again, to play the consultant role. Instead of saying, "You need to get these grades up / have a clean room / sleep nine hours each night," start the conversation by expressing empathy. "I know that this situation isn't bothering you, and you may be right that it's not that big a deal. It feels like a bigger deal to me, though, and I'm wondering if we can figure out a way of looking at this that works for both of us. It would help me if I knew what kind of goals make sense to you around schoolwork/cleanliness/sleep. And it will also help me think clearly about the limits that are really important to me, because I don't want to allow you to do things that would cause me to become resentful."

That doesn't mean you have *no* say in your child's choices. You are still the parent. But if you start from a place of believing that:

1. Your child wants their life to work out, and

2. You can't *make* them do anything they really don't want to do, and thus you can't be responsible for accomplishing the impossible

. . . then changing the energy percentages seems logical and safe to do.

Try stepping back, and then fill in the chart on the next page. It might be that it seems like the total percentage is then 10 percent or 20 percent—meaning, the task isn't getting done. That doesn't mean it isn't working. In fact, it means it *is* working, as it is showing your child that it is their life, and that if they want a particular element of it to work better for them, they need to step up.

> It is more important for a child to develop a clear sense of who's responsible for what than for them always to do well.

ISSUE	PERCENTAGE OF ENERGY YOU AND OTHERS (NOT YOUR CHILD) PLAN TO GIVE	PERCENTAGE OF ENERGY YOU WANT YOUR CHILD TO GIVE	TOTAL PERCENT
Zack's screen time usage.	Twenty-five percent. We will check in through regular conversations about how screens are being used and work with Zack to create realistic guidelines. In certain situations, we'll eliminate screens for a while to create space for Zack to get important tasks done.	Fifty percent. Zack will experiment with different reminder styles, will share victories and slip-ups, and invite us to help him shape boundaries around screen usage.	Seventy-five percent. This reflects that screen usage is an important variable in our family dynamic and Zack's development, but it's not our only priority and we're going to hold it a bit more lightly.

The Emotions of the Parent Consultant

Because the word "consultant" comes from the business world, it may seem like a removed or objective role—and even emotionally less fraught than "manager." In fact, being a parent consultant is incredibly tough emotionally (but it pays well!). It means you have to give up some control, which is hard for all the reasons we outlined in the Introduction. It means you have to watch your child make mistakes and watch as they struggle to correct them. It means that you try not to feel sorry for them because you don't want them to feel sorry for themselves or send them the message that they're not capable of handling challenges. You want to model a courageous approach to setbacks, after all. In other words, this whole consultant business is no picnic, and while it's one thing to *know* it's the right thing to do, staying the course is a different beast.

Our goal is to convince parents—and *you*, dear reader—that it *is* safe. How do we know it is? Countless readers tell us that it saved their relationship with their child. And there are decades of scientific research that support the importance of a sense of control and the problems caused by parental over-control, as well as research that has documented the very slow maturation of the prefrontal cortex. And our own personal experience as kids, and as parents. And our relationships with thousands of families. It is safe to hand more control to your child. We promise.

Exercise: What Gets In Your Way

Think about the following scenarios:

An eleven-year-old being supported to decide what bedtime makes the most sense for her.

An eight-year-old being supported to decide when to do his homework.

A fourteen-year-old making her own choice about whether to attend a public school or a private school.

A nine-year-old refusing to get help with reading, even though he is behind and his teacher says he needs extra help.

A seventeen-year-old making an ill-advised decision not to apply to any safety schools for college, and refusing to consider advice from people who have much more experience than he has.

▶ Would it be hard for you not to push for the outcome you want?

_____

_____

_____

▶ Why?

_____

_____

_____

▶ Is your reasoning logical or is your reaction rooted in fear?

_____

_____

_____

▶ If you go back to the principle that your child wants their life to work out, does anything change in your feelings about these scenarios?

_____

_____

_____

▶ Do you believe your child would consistently make choices that are worse than the ones you or another adult would make for them?

_____

_____

_____

▶ Is it so terrible for kids to regret some of the decisions they make—and to learn from them?

_____

_____

_____

When kids bring you their problems, remember to ask yourself, "Whose problem is it?"

The Myth of the Good Parent

When we've talked to parents about what makes the consultant model difficult for them, we've learned that some of the struggle is fear of their child floundering, and some of it is fear of how they themselves will be perceived by other parents. A set of myths exists about what it means to be a good parent, and those expectations create pressure for parents to intervene when really, for everyone's sake, they shouldn't. Here are some of the most common myths about good parenting:

Myth: A good parent's child is always well-behaved in public.

Myth: A good parent stays on their kids to make sure they get good grades.

Myth: A good parent makes their kid clean their room.

Myth: A good parent makes sure their kid goes to school in clean, weather-appropriate clothes (matching is a bonus).

Myth: A good parent makes sure their kid eats all the food groups each day, and not too much sugar.

Myth: A good parent has kids who are nice to their siblings.

Myth: A good parent has kids who are always respectful of authority.

Myth: A good parent always knows where their kid is by tracking them with Life360 or a similar app.

Now, we can offer you story after story of children we know who behaved poorly in public, got terrible grades, kept a sloppy room, wore inappropriate clothes, ate nothing but chips, terrorized their siblings, and acted out against authority . . . and then went on to be wonderful, healthy adults with loving families and fulfilling careers, and are motivated to give back to their communities. Sometimes these anecdotes are comforting. And sometimes they aren't enough. Frequently when we encourage parents to let kids make their own decisions, they'll say to us, quietly, "If I did that, other parents/teachers/coaches would think I wasn't doing my job." Parents worry about being judged by other parents when their kid shows up in shorts on a cold day, or by teachers when their kid doesn't turn in their work (because the parents didn't monitor their assignments on the school's portal). And they're not wrong to worry about this—they probably *are* being judged, just as they themselves probably judge other parents, and teachers, too.

But the plain truth is that, good parent or bad parent, there's much we don't control because *some kids are a lot easier than others.* Some kids come out of the womb low-key and able to adapt to their environment, while others are rigid, overly sensitive, and reactive, or just plain *hard.* Some kids will naturally strive for good grades and to please their teachers, while other kids will naturally rebel against any adult who tells them what to do. That doesn't mean that parents have *no* role to play, and certainly if their kid is a monster to their teacher, we're not suggesting a parent shrug their shoulders and say, "He just came out that way." Indeed, while we can't control our kids, we can control what we are willing to do—and not do—for them. It doesn't make sense to pay for college if a kid hasn't shown they're ready, for instance. Or to drive all over town taking him to guitar lessons when he isn't practicing or making any progress. You can't make him practice, and you shouldn't—but you also don't have to put energy into something that he's showing he doesn't really care about.

Everyone can understand that some kids have more challenges than others, and also that some periods of life are more challenging than others. We know many parents who feel like failures because they have a troubled or very difficult child, even though they have two or three other children who are successful and well-adjusted, and who were parented in the same way.

For those who fear the consultant model because of the judgment of others, we'd like to pose a question to help you release the worry: *When* do we judge whether someone is a good parent? When their child is a rambunctious toddler? A surly tween? A wild teenager? When they're admitted to a top college? Or when they take a medical leave halfway through college because they're so burned out? A confused adult? It's a rhetorical question because of course the answer is that we don't, or rather, we shouldn't. If you're stuck in a self-critical loop because your child is struggling, remember that judging parents because of the conduct of their children, at any age, is a waste of time and energy—and one never knows the full picture. We've worked with dozens and dozens of parents who were worried and critical of themselves because their children were struggling but whose children turned out to do extremely well.

When our kids behave poorly, it's easy to blame ourselves, and it's easy to assume other parents are blaming us. It's hard work to change that framing, but it's important. And we speak from experience. There's nothing that throws that judgment pressure into starker relief than when you're a "parenting expert"! After *The Self-Driven Child* was published, Ned had some really challenging times with his kids, in ways that were surely apparent to others. It was easy for Ned to think, *Can I really be a credible parenting author? Everything is hard!* But the reframing of that thought process is: *The fact that my kids are struggling is not evidence that I'm not a good parent. In fact, thank goodness I know some of the stuff I know about parenting because otherwise this would be so much harder.*

Exercise: Responding to Judgers

Let's assume that you're having a conversation with a friend who can be a bit judgmental. They have just made a comment about a crop top your child is wearing and noted that they refuse to let their child wear such shirts. Here's a range of responses:

A. Agree and change your perspective: "I know—I'm never letting her wear that top again!"

B. Ignore and move on: "Oh, thanks for sharing. Hey, did you see the Cubs game last night?"

C. Go on the defensive: "I want her to be free to make her own choices as long as what she's doing isn't dangerous or disrespectful, and wearing a crop top to the mall isn't either."

D. Be proactive, and call out the judgment: "Well, different rules for different families. We never really know what's gone into other people's decisions."

Which approach feels most comfortable to you? Why?

_____

_____

_____

Naturally, what you're comfortable with will change depending on how close you are with your friend. Some people might want to call out the judgment, in the moment or at a later time, but it really is dependent on your personality and the nature of the friendship.

Bringing It Home: The Reality of a Good Parent

When you think about how you will judge yourself when you look back years from now, what do you think will be most important to you about being a parent? What will it mean for you to have done a good (or, to use the phrase coined by child psychiatrist Donald Winnicott, a "good enough") job? How will you know?

_____

_____

_____

_____

_____

_____

_____

_____

_____

 **Cross-Check:**

Principle 1—_Put Connection First_

Principle 5—_Motivate Your Kids Without Trying to Change Them_

Principle 6—_Be a Nonanxious Presence in Your Family_

PRINCIPLE 3

Communicate
Healthy Expectations

When Bill had a psychotherapy practice early in his career, he asked new adult clients what they were hoping to get out of therapy. A strikingly high percentage said something like, "I feel like I've spent the first thirty-eight years of my life trying to live up to other people's expectations. Now I'm trying to figure out what's important to me and how I want to live."

We all have expectations of ourselves, our partners, our friends, and our colleagues. We certainly have expectations of our kids, and it's been shown that both parental and teacher expectations strongly influence academic outcomes. It's also been shown, however, that excessive pressure to excel is the fourth-leading cause of adolescent unwellness (behind only poverty, trauma, and discrimination), and that rising parental expectations as kids move toward the college years are strongly associated with perfectionism.

But I don't put pressure on my kids, you might be thinking. And you may not. Interestingly, though, kids' self-imposed pressure not to disappoint their parents seems to create more stress than the actual pressure they experience from their parents. Kids want their parents to be proud of them, and research implies that, even if parents aren't saying anything, or even if they think they aren't communicating pressure, kids are still getting the message about achievement—and worry about letting their parents down.

It's pretty rare that we take time to probe what it means to have expectations of others. For example, if a parent says to a child, "I expect you to . . . ," does it mean that:

1. I anticipate that you will,

2. I am confident that you can, or

3. I insist that you do . . . or else there will be consequences.

It's also rare that we carefully consider exactly what our expectations are, where they're coming from, and if everyone has the same understanding of them. This particular consideration is important because, based on research and what we hear from students, even if your kids seem to tune you out, even if you suspect they don't care what you think, they actually do care. They want you to believe in them, and many of the kids we see give up on themselves because they think that they will always be a disappointment to their parents. It makes sense, then, to put care into setting the right kind of expectations, to make sure everyone is on the same page, and to communicate expectations in a way that will instill confidence rather than add stress and pressure.

While most of the exercises in this book are designed for you to do alone or with your partner, this chapter is a little different. We recommend that you involve your kids if they're open to it, as so much of the work involves clarifying what your kids interpret to be your expectations of them, and your understanding of their expectations of themselves.

Note that while there are many kinds of expectations (surrounding behavior, chores, academics, extracurriculars, religion, relationships, and more), the particular type we want to address in this book are those tied to *achievement*. By achievement, we mean external accomplishments—things like rushing yards or goals, student council elections, and, of course, grades, test scores, and college admissions. For the record, we think achievement is a good thing, and we've always felt happy about our own kids' accomplishments, and our own. It's just that kids' achievements feel hollow to them if they're sought primarily to impress a parent or to avoid punishment or embarrassment.

Let's dig in:

▶ What expectations around academic achievement do you have for your kids? What about expectations for success in extracurriculars? Do you expect your kids to get good grades, to work their hardest, to achieve at a high level in sports or other extracurriculars? Or merely to participate? Or do you even expect them to participate?

_____

_____

_____

▶ Do you expect that your kids will absolutely go to college? An elite one?

_____

_____

_____

▶ Do you have a plan or career in mind for your child? A level of income? A lifestyle?

_____

_____

_____

▶ Now, explore what you mean when you say you have expectations for your kids: Do you mean (1) "I anticipate that you will," (2) "I am confident that you can," or (3) "I insist that you do . . . or else there will be consequences"?

_____

_____

_____

▶ How do you think you communicate these expectations to your kids? What language—verbal or nonverbal—do you think you use?

_____

_____

_____

▶ Now, ask your kids: What do they *think* your expectations for them are?

_____

_____

_____

Reflection questions:

▶ Is there a difference between what you expect and what your kids think you expect?

_____

_____

_____

▶ If so, why might that be?

_____

_____

_____

The Guiding Rules of Expectations

In this next section, we set some guideposts for expectations—things that we've found to be true in our own lives and in our work, and also that decades of research have supported. After each one, we offer an exercise to help you explore it further.

HEALTHY EXPECTATIONS ARE SET BY COMMUNICATING A HIGH DEGREE OF CONFIDENCE IN YOUR CHILD'S ABILITY TO ACHIEVE RATHER THAN BY INSISTING OR REQUIRING THAT THEY PERFORM AT A CERTAIN LEVEL.

We know that parental expectations can be a powerful force for good. When a parent or a teacher conveys that they believe in a child, and in the child's abilities, that affirmation cuts through self-doubt and negative stereotyping that could otherwise hold them back. For decades, we've known that kids learn and perform best in an environment that offers high challenge but low threat. When expectations are expressed as "I'm confident that you can do really well if it's important to you," the language increases kids' self-confidence and motivates them to work hard because it conveys belief in their ability to rise to challenges but is not threatening. In contrast, when expectations are expressed as "I know you could do well if you only cared," kids see a guilt trip and a minefield of disappointment. Language like "You need to do well or I'm taking away your . . ." feels threatening, as it implies that they may be loved conditionally—that their parents will be disappointed, won't be proud of them, or will be angry at them if they don't meet the expectation. It's also coercive, and undermines a kid's sense of control. It implies that what's important to us is more critical than what's important to them. Many kids have even told us that they interpret this kind of expectation to mean that their parents care more about their achievement than they do about them as people. And here's the thing: Language matters a lot. The line between conveying high confidence (healthy expectations) and conveying a sense of threat (toxic expectations) is much finer than you might imagine.

A great way to express confidence but not pressure to your child is to say, "I believe you can."

Exercise: Language Watch

Sometimes, parents communicate unhealthy pressure and expectations indirectly. Look at the phrases below and see if you've used them, or something along the same lines. Note that most parents have, so don't be too hard on yourself.

"Why would you want to play recreational soccer this year when you could be on a travel team?"

"Your sister's knocking it out of the park."

"If you'd just spent a little more time studying for the placement exam, you could have gotten into the advanced math class."

"It looked like you weren't giving it your all today."

"You could do it if you put in even a little bit of effort."

"You need to do better in science or it will ruin your GPA."

"If you don't get those grades up, no college is going to want you."

Take stock of the language you've used in the past. Most parents who do hold the "demanding" form of expectations do so out of love and the desire to see their child have every possible advantage in life. Remember, it's okay if you have used some of these phrases! Realistically, most parents have. But be honest with yourself. What are some phrases that upon reflection you recognize as being pressuring?

For a week, pay close attention to the expectation-setting language you use around your child. If you catch yourself using pressuring language, write it down. If you find yourself feeling impatient or frustrated, make a note. What did you say? How did you say it? Why do you *think* you said it? Were you feeling stressed or anxious? Or were you just not particularly careful with your words, even though you didn't mean anything by it? What could you have said instead?

_____

_____

_____

_____

_____

_____

_____

_____

_____

Tell your child you're working hard not to use language that makes them feel pressured, or that makes them think that you'll love them less if they don't do well. Ask them to call you out on things you say that, to them, convey pressure. If they call you on it, write it down. What did you say that upset them? What did you mean by what you said? What was going on with you when you said it?

_____

_____

_____

_____

_____

_____

_____

_____

_____

Note that kids can certainly handle some parental pressure. They won't be damaged for life if they sometimes feel that you want them to work harder or perform better than they currently are—or to care more about something than they presently do. In fact, handling pressure successfully can build resilience. But remember that chronic excessive pressure to excel really hurts kids, who do much better emotionally if they know they are loved and respected by their parents no matter what and aren't continually burdened by crippling expectations of the "achieve or else" kind.

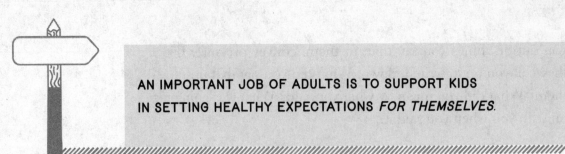

We have seen countless kids look at us blankly when we ask them what goals and expectations they have for themselves. "Tune out every voice but your own," we say. "What do *you* want?"

"I don't really know," they often say, "I've never thought about it."

When we push them further as to why that is, they often share a variation of "I'm too busy trying to meet everyone else's expectations." And that "everyone else"? It's parents, sure, but it's also their peers, their teachers, their coaches, their unrealistic social media role models, and their spiritual leaders. But when we think about the kind of kids we want to send out into the world, it's kids who've been listening to their own voice for a long time about what's important to them, what it is they want, how to get it, and how to handle it if it's a swing and a miss.

Our role as adults is to support our kids, to help them set self-expectations that are reasonable, to caution them when they're not reasonable, and to put the whole goal/expectations game in perspective. A goal is something you deeply want to achieve—as opposed to a demand, which is something you think you must achieve in order to maintain your sense of self-worth and emotional well-being.

For example, if the two of us set out to write two books in

the next two years, that would be a solid long-term goal. In fact, it would be considered what's called a SMART goal because it's Specific, Measurable, Attainable (most likely), Realistic, and Time-Bound. If we were to have healthy expectations of ourselves, we would anticipate that we could indeed do it because we are pretty awesome, capable, and have a lot of support. What's more, *we* chose the goal—it didn't come from our agent or editor or anyone else. If, however, we felt that *not* writing two books in two years would make us failures, or that other people wouldn't love or appreciate us, then the expectation would be toxic.

While certainly some parents and teachers contribute to toxic expectations, we also want to be clear that kids are more than capable of setting unhealthy expectations all on their own! In a recent study of students in three high-achieving suburban high schools, "pressure from self" was consistently rated as the number-one stressor. Our job, then, is to help kids find their way to the right way of thinking.

Exercise: Clarifying Self-Expectations and Goals

Have a conversation with your child in which you ask them to answer some questions either in a journal, if they'd prefer, or in a casual conversation. You could start the conversation by saying something like, "I've been reading about expectations that parents have for kids and that kids have for themselves. It's completely up to you, but I'd love to get a better idea of the kinds of things you expect of yourself. Is it okay if I ask you some questions?"

And now, here are the questions:

- What academic expectations do you have for yourself? What kind of grades, test scores, etc.? Where does this expectation come from? Do you feel that you *can* do this, or that you *should* do it? Do you feel you're *capable* of it, or that you *must* do it? Do you feel that other people *expect* you to do it?

_____

_____

_____

- What expectations do you have for yourself about your extracurricular activities? For instance, do you want to try one new thing? Two? Be engaged in a club at a higher level? Is there a level you're hoping to reach in Scouting, for instance, or a goal you have for your journalism club? Do you want to make the varsity team as a junior or get a singing role in the musical?

_____

_____

_____

- What about with your friends? How do you expect yourself to show up in your friendships?

_____

_____

_____

- What other expectations do you think about? Do you have expectations regarding your relationship with your family? In your alone time? For your community? This could be things like helping with the cooking, or trying to read a new series, or visiting your grandmother regularly.

_____

_____

_____

- Of what's listed, what's the most important to you? Why?

_____

_____

_____

- If you didn't reach a goal, I'd guess you'd be disappointed, but how much of that would be about not getting to do the thing, and how much of it would be turned inward? (Frustration with yourself?) How would you cope with that?

_____

_____

_____

- How much of your disappointment would be about a fear of letting others down?

_____

_____

_____

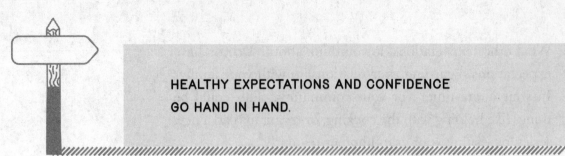

We can't talk about expectations without also talking about confidence. If someone is feeling uncertain and struggling with self-esteem, they are much less likely to set healthy expectations for themselves, or to find the drive to reach those expectations. If your kid is in this camp, there's a lot you can do to help them "trick their brain" into having the sense of competency they need to pursue their goals.

Exercise: Training a Confident Brain

Start, as always, by trying to gain their buy-in. Tell them, "I'd love to know what you feel confident about and what you don't—and if there are some things you'd like to feel more confident about. Is this something we can talk about?"

If they say no, leave it be. But it's very possible they will return to you later to revisit the topic.

If they say yes, ask: "Would you like to train your brain to expect yourself to do well?"

Assuming that they say yes, say: "I hear it helps to write down as many times as you can remember the times when you've gotten positive feedback about an achievement or about you as a person—and times that you've felt like you'd done something really well." It may be little stuff, like an aunt praising them for being so good with their younger cousins, getting the lead in a class production as a third grader, a coach telling them they're a good team player, or a time when they made a meal for the family that everyone loved. It can also be bigger things like writing a paper on which they got good feedback, performing successfully at a debate, solving a math problem that most kids couldn't get, or not giving up on a hard-to-achieve goal (like dunking a basketball).

_____

_____

_____

_____

_____

_____

_____

Now, it's your turn as a steady adult in their life to add to this list—surely there are things they've forgotten!

_____

_____

_____

_____

_____

_____

Keep this list—and, for that matter, make a similar one for yourself! Encourage your child to add to it and to look at it before embarking on a challenge, or when they're having a crappy day and are feeling bad about themselves.

We know this can help. When Bill started his neuropsychologist practice, he didn't know if he would be successful or not. (Maybe because he got fired from his first job as a neuropsychologist!) In addition to making a list like the one in the exercise, Bill used a lot of positive self-talk, telling himself things like "I can be really good at this" and "I know a lot of ways to help people." He also kept a list of all the kids he tested or saw for psychotherapy, on which he'd put an up arrow (↑) if he was sure he helped them, or a down arrow (↓) if he wasn't sure or felt that he hadn't. To his great satisfaction, he saw that he was helping at least 90 percent of the kids he was seeing. After he saw this month after month for a year or so, he didn't have to make the list anymore. Bill also remembers that after he flunked out of graduate school the first time he went (for not turning in any work) and was considering trying it again, he read and reread a couple of letters of recommendation that his college professors had written for him in order to build his confidence.

Because Bill knew from his own personal experience how powerful the words of confidence voiced by others are, he has always followed up his testing of older children and adolescents with a session in which he tells them what he learned about them. Before the meeting, he writes out all of the things they're good at, then nice things about them as a person, and then the two or three areas that are more challenging and could use attention. At the end of the session, he asks the kids to keep the written summary in their rooms, to read it from time to time to remind them what they're capable of, and, when they experience setbacks, to read it over and over to regain their confidence. Bill has former clients—now full-grown adults—who have kept the list in their rooms for twenty years.

This approach works for adults too. We have a friend who is constantly having to put herself out there to gain new business, which takes a lot of confidence, stamina, and the ability to tolerate rejection. On days when it feels hard, she brings out a file where she has saved compliments and accolades she's received over the years. It helps her remember that she knows her stuff, and that if she stays the course, she'll do well. It helps her remember: "This is who I am—capable and confident."

Exercise: Praise Letter

Write a letter to your child. Tell them what you notice about them. Are they a leader? An empath? A hard worker? What do you see as their strengths? Be specific by backing up your perspective with anecdotes or references to shared experiences. Acknowledge that you know they struggle with certain things, and what those things are. But emphasize that you see them growing, and encourage them to be patient with themselves. If possible, emphasize any area in their life in which they work really hard. So you can say that you love the fact that they work hard to get better and better at—and do a good job in—the things that are important to them. Suggest that they keep the letter somewhere safe, where they can refer to it if they are having a hard time. Granted, a letter from a parent carries different weight than a letter from a more objective third party. But that can also make it *more* powerful.

If you're a teacher, this letter can take the form of a letter of recommendation, or even notes on a report card.

Exercise: Remember What Really Matters

We want our kids to feel great about what they can do, of course, but we also want them to know that they are much more than their accomplishments, which can help them in all manner of ways. Studies have shown, for example, that if students write a paragraph about what they value most before taking a test, they experience less anxiety and perform better on the test—presumably because it helps them keep the importance of the test in perspective. And so, once you're done listing the amazing things your child has done in their short life, as well as the wonderful things about them as human beings, bring the conversation back to *values*. In this next exercise, ask them if they'll list some values that are important to them. It could be things like friendship, integrity, family, loyalty, reliability, or community-mindedness, or it could be athletic or academic success. No judgment. Then, after the value, ask them to write a sentence about—or at least think about— why it's important to them.

Value:

_____

_____

Why it's important to me:

_____

_____

Value:

_____

_____

Why it's important to me:

_____

_____

Value:

_____

_____

Why it's important to me:

_____

_____

Value:

_____

_____

Why it's important to me:

_____

_____

Value:

_____

_____

Why it's important to me:

_____

_____

HEALTHY EXPECTATIONS DON'T COEXIST WITH PERFECTIONISM.

You could put absolutely no pressure on your child, and they could still live as if they are being chased by the accomplishment police. Some people are born this way. Perfectionists tend to be very bright, black-and-white thinkers who rigidly internalize a world of toxic expectations around them. They are high achievers who put an enormous amount of pressure on themselves to succeed in all things, no matter what; who strenuously avoid or mask mistakes and perceived failures; and who feel that less-than-perfect equals complete failure. It's tricky because many in our culture perceive perfectionism as an admirable quality and even reward it—think of the honor bestowed on valedictorians who, by definition, excel in every subject. But in reality it's a dangerous quality that's correlated with anxiety, depression, obsessive-compulsive disorder, and anorexia—and with relatively low success in adult life compared to those who are motivated to perform at a high level but do not see mistakes and finishing in second place as equaling total failure.

We want our kids to seek excellence, naturally, but there's a difference between someone who is motivated to achieve their goals because of the satisfaction that excellent performance brings—and a perfectionist. An excellence-seeker has high standards, but also has self-compassion and causes much less collateral damage for themselves and others. An excellence-seeker doesn't love mistakes but sees them as a way to grow. Excellence-seekers are more intrinsically motivated and, interestingly, the "error-detection" function in their brains is more active, as they are eager to notice—and to learn from—their mistakes. Perfectionists, on the other hand, are so averse to making mistakes that they don't attend to them as much—their brains tune out mistakes instead of growing from them.

Excellence-Seeker	Perfectionist
I need to be open about my mistakes so I can learn from them.	I have to hide my mistakes.
Everyone is wrong sometimes—it's okay. At least I'm out there trying.	It's not okay to be wrong. People will think less of me if I'm not the best.
I still have a lot to learn, and that's okay.	If I don't figure this out, everyone will think I'm stupid.
I want to be really excellent at this. I'd like to be the best, and one day I might be. But I also recognize there are a lot of people who are really talented—I can learn from them.	I have to be the best at this. This is who I am.
It's not really anyone's business if I didn't get a top score, but I'm not ashamed of it either.	I don't want anyone to know unless I get a perfect score.
Failure isn't fun, but it can be motivating.	Failure, which means less than perfect, is terrifying—and is not an option.
I'm grateful for people who are smarter than me—they may be able to make important contributions to the world. And I'm smart enough to do something meaningful and important too.	If someone's better than me in math (or anything else), it means I suck at it, and I hope nobody knows.
I scored in the ninety-first percentile on that test—that's pretty darn good!	I'm ashamed I scored in the ninety-first percentile because it means that other kids did better than I did.

Exercise: Wrestling with Perfectionism

You probably have a good sense from the chart above if you are dealing with a perfectionist child. But here are some questions to ask them to clarify how significant a problem it might be.

▶ Does not being the best at something make you feel like a failure?

_____

_____

▶ Do you ruminate about past failures?

_____

_____

▶ Does making mistakes make you feel ashamed?

_____

_____

▶ Do you often feel let down by people who don't perform as you wanted them to?

_____

_____

▶ Are you worried that other people will think less of you if you make mistakes or aren't the best?

_____

_____

▶ Do you find it hard to hear feedback from others?

_____

_____

▶ If fear of not being the best wasn't always chasing you, do you feel that you wouldn't do well in life?

_____

_____

▶ Do you feel like your fears of failing or making mistakes keep you from trying new things?

_____

_____

Now, turn the lens around and ask the questions of yourself.

If you are a perfectionist, start there, with you. How have you minimized these tendencies and increased your self-compassion?

_____

_____

_____

_____

_____

_____

_____

_____

_____

If you see perfectionism in your child, what can you do about it? It's a tough one because, as we say in Principle 5, you can't change your child if your child doesn't want your help to change. And it's counterproductive to try, as many perfectionists feel threatened by any attempt to help them lighten up a bit. What you can do is help them see why they might want to make changes themselves. Toward that end, you could say:

"I know you really expect a lot from yourself, and I'm not trying to take that away from you. I notice, though, that you're awfully hard on yourself when you don't do the absolute best at everything, and I suspect that being so hard on yourself actually holds you back. Do you ever think that?" If they say yes, you can ask, "Is that something you'd like to be different?"

If they say yes, hooray! While it won't be something that changes overnight, you can show them the grid above that stacks perfectionists against excellence-seekers. Tear it out of the book, or recreate it and put it somewhere they can frequently see it. In our experience, if we let perfectionists know that we aren't suggesting they become slackers and, in fact, want them to work hard and perform well at things that are important to them, it can make them feel that it's safe to modify some of their rigid attitudes about achievement and success. Attitudes take time and practice to change, but you're in a great starting place if they like the idea of performing at a high level without torturing themselves when they aren't always the best.

If they say no, the best thing you can do is model the self-compassion and growth mindset you'd like them to have. Without explicitly indicating that you're trying to teach your child a different way of looking at things, you can do this by sharing stories about mistakes you've made or times you've failed, and how you felt badly about it at first but that it ended up okay and that you really learned from it. You can tell stories about the ups and downs of grandparents, or historical figures, to help give your child greater context for how failures shape a person. You can send them an article about perfectionists vs. excellence-seekers and simply say, "You may be interested in this."

And you can emphasize a focus on one's personal best. They don't have control over who gets a better score or is cast in the lead or elevated to varsity. But they do have control over their own improvement over time and with effort, and that's what should be emphasized and celebrated.

Exercise: Honoring Mistakes and Failures as Necessary Steps on the Road to Success

Over dinner, on a walk, or in the car, brainstorm with your child about a time each of you has made a mistake or did poorly on something that ended up leading to a cool opportunity.

Now, think together of other people's mistakes that they've grown from. It could be your spouse, or a teacher. It could be that kid who messed up in the piano concert that one time. It could be an athlete who didn't qualify for the Olympics but came back to competition stronger than ever, and became an example to athletes everywhere of how it's okay to come up short. It could be a character on a favorite TV show or book. Examples of failure-as-character-building are everywhere in pop culture. The whole genre of inspirational sports movies wouldn't exist without them!

FAQ: Okay, BUT . . .

What about the underachievers? I have a kid who is probably the smartest in his class, but he just stopped trying once he got to high school.

It could be that school just isn't a priority for him, and, believe it or not, there's nothing wrong with that. Many successful people cared more about sports, music, drama, dance, debate, or their friends than they did about school, and most of them went on to lead successful and satisfying lives.

If kids aren't bothered by their underachievement, we want to remind ourselves to ask, "Whose problem is it?" and not try to solve someone else's problem or catastrophize the future. There are hundreds of influences on kids' lives that can turn things around, including a girlfriend who doesn't want a slacker boyfriend, a teacher who gives them positive feedback and expresses confidence in their abilities, the realization that they won't be able to play soccer on the school team if they don't get their grades up, or simply the maturation of the prefrontal cortex, which allows kids and young adults to be much more focused on—and realistic about—their future.

If kids *are* bothered by not doing well, ideally we can have them evaluated by a neuropsychologist to see if they have any learning difficulties that are affecting them. If they are struggling because they can't make themselves work hard enough to do better, an evaluation can clarify whether they may have ADHD (and thus lower levels of dopamine, the neurotransmitter for drive) and/or a problem with anxiety, the major manifestation of which is avoidance of things that make us anxious. In our experience, these are the two main reasons that kids don't work hard—even when they want to.

Expectation Fallacies

We tend to hear the same concerns from parents again and again when it comes to expectations. We love getting pushback because it helps us deepen the conversation and get to the heart of some of the most basic misconceptions we all have about what it means to live up to our potential, to try our best, and the reality of the world we live in. Here are some of the most common objections we hear, and our responses.

> *"It's important to me that my child always does their best."*

If you really stop and think about it, do *you* always do your best? In all things? Or do you pick and choose where to give effort, and how much of it to give? It probably isn't always your best! Ned does his best when he's first meeting with a family—he wants to pay close attention to the parents, their child, and their dynamics, and he gives his best when having sensitive conversations. But when he's going through the Pythagorean theorem for the seventeenth time in a day with a student, he's likely not giving his absolute best.

Bill does his best when he gives kids feedback about themselves, when he writes reports, when he sings and plays music, and when he talks to his children or grandchildren about sensitive topics. He doesn't intentionally try to do a mediocre job of anything, but, professionally, there's much he can do on autopilot. He knows if he tried to be outstanding at everything he did, it wouldn't be an effective use of energy.

The point is, we couldn't possibly operate at "our best" one hundred percent of the time. So why would we expect our kids to?

> *"My child is really intelligent/athletic/talented, and if they don't work hard, it feels like such a waste of their talent and a lost opportunity."*

This comment gets at the fear of lost potential. But the reality is that kids reach their full potential when they work hard at something they're passionate about and create a satisfying life. Just because they are good at, say, playing the piano, doesn't mean that they should pursue it to the best of their ability if they don't love it. Think of it as an opportunity cost—what else could they be spending time on that they're great at *and* that they love? People don't reach their full potential by being pushed all the time—they burn out that way. As we've said, research has shown us again and again that while pressure might work for the short term, it doesn't work in the long term and can jeopardize your relationship with your child.

> *"I don't want my child to ever feel pressured by me, so I say very little about their achievements."*

Silence can be interpreted as *dis*approval, and kids have been known to push themselves just to try to get some praise. If you're concerned about inadvertently putting pressure on them when you praise them, you might say, "You really wanted that and worked hard for it. In my opinion, you have every right to be proud of yourself!" That would keep the focus on their expectations for themselves, and not your expectations for them.

> *"The reality is that we live in a competitive world—people will always have expectations of my child, and I need to set the bar high to make sure they have a good life."*

This statement comes from a mindset about the world that is fearful, and also one that suggests that a "good life" is one coated with outward signs of achievement. A bar that some-

one else sets for your child is never going to be as meaningful as the bar they set for themselves.

Let's play with a scenario around expectations. We've
laid out several possible responses to the scenario. Select
which one you think conveys healthy expectations.

> Kids don't maximize their potential by being continually pushed. They maximize their potential by creating a life that they're happy with.

Scenario

Your son runs cross-country and is good enough that
he's qualified for the state competition. You're really excited
for him, as he's trained hard all season. The week before the
race, you notice your son has made a lot of social plans in the
evenings. It worries you because you can see that he won't be
rested enough to compete well. Do you:

A. Say "I know you have this big meet this weekend and
that your social calendar is pretty full. I also know
that both of these things are important, and that I
don't know what's best for you. I'm confident you can
make a good decision for yourself, and I want you
to practice making this kind of decision because I
want you to learn to assess your life and learn to
trust yourself. I'm available if you want to talk it
through."

B. Point out that if he does all of these activities, he will
likely be tired and probably not perform his best, and
so prohibit him from going out so much.

C. Say nothing—it's his life, and his race.

D. Email his coach and see what kind of guidance they have or if they might intervene.

As this is the *end* of the chapter, not the beginning, you probably have gleaned that we'd opt for **Option A**. It's respectful of the competing attentions of the child's life, and avoids putting your thumb on the scale of how important the track meet is. It also acknowledges that your son needs practice making decisions, and encourages him to tune in to his inner motivation.

Our concern with **Option B** is that, going back to the language of expectations, it suggests that he *must* perform his best, and that that expectation comes from you, not him.

> It's dangerous to give a teenager the message that you know better than they do and that they should trust your judgment rather than their own.

Saying nothing at all, as in **Option C**, doesn't allow the opportunity for a dialogue that could be really helpful to your child and open the door to healthy communication between you two as you guide him to set healthy expectations for himself.

And emailing the coach, as in **Option D**, is simply too meddlesome. If your son is really conflicted, you might suggest that *he* email the coach himself for guidance about how he should approach the week before a meet. But remember: It's your son's life, not yours.

 **Cross-Check:**

Principle 1—*Put Connection First*

Principle 2—*Be a Consultant, Not a Boss or Manager*

Principle 5—*Motivate Your Kids Without Trying to Change Them*

Principle 6—*Be a Nonanxious Presence in Your Family*

4

Teach Your Kids an Accurate Model of Reality

What do you want most for your child as they grow into an adult? Rate each of the below with a number between 1 and 4, where 4 = *really important*, 3 = *somewhat important*, 2 = *not too important but would be nice*, and 1 = *I don't really care*:

- [ ] academic and/or career success
- [ ] financial success
- [ ] close friendships
- [ ] honesty and integrity
- [ ] happiness and fulfillment
- [ ] marriage
- [ ] fame
- [ ] prestige
- [ ] power
- [ ] children of their own
- [ ] a close relationship with you

We're going to direct you back to this page later, but you have to read on to find out why.

Since completing our second book, we've been giving a talk

to groups of high school students called "Creating a Life You Want." The focus of the talk is on ways that kids can take control of their own lives by identifying what's important to them and working hard in the service of their self-development. In other words, we talk to them about how to create a life that they'll be happy with—because we want them to be happy. It turns out that, while kids shouldn't be protected from all possible stresses and challenges, being happy is a really good thing at any age. Happy people obviously feel better than unhappy people, but they also do better, in the sense that they have better relationships, find more career and financial success, have better health, and live longer. In fact, some of the wisest people on the planet have even taught that happiness is actually the whole point of being. Aristotle said, "Happiness is the meaning and purpose of life, the whole aim and end of human existence." The Dalai Lama said, "The very purpose of life is to be happy."

The problem is that kids are *not* very happy. As we mentioned, anxiety and depression in children, teens, and young adults are currently at record levels. We suspect that this is related, at least in part, to young people growing up with very high levels of stress based on, in significant part, an inaccurate model of reality. Most of the kids we've spoken to in recent years—and many of their parents—seem to believe that the most important outcome of their entire childhood and adolescence is where they go to college. Most also believe that the road to success is extremely narrow, that there are a very limited number of career options, that kids who aren't top students have no chance at success, that few second chances are available, and that prestige and money inevitably lead to happiness.

It's true that, for people with means, second chances *are* more available than for those with a low income, and we don't want to discount the role of privilege, especially for those living on small margins. But on the whole, many parents fear falling off a narrow path that, for their kids, is actually not very narrow at all.

We don't think the narrow path reflects an accurate model of reality, even as we understand why kids (and many parents) feel this way. Parents are fearful about a shrinking middle class; they're fearful about failure; they're fearful that their kids aren't fearful *enough*. Parents aren't telling their kids that the road to success is narrow *just* to scare them. They're telling them that because they think it's so. And they think it's so because they're caught in a maelstrom of other anxious parents who know that Stanford used to accept 20 percent of its applicants and now accepts only 4 percent. Or that it used to be that you could get into the University of Washington with a 2.5 GPA, but now you need a 3.75. Or that a college education used to be affordable but now requires a scholarship or a spot at a competitive state school where tuition will be manageable.

We don't deny that there can be some advantages to going to elite colleges. If you want to be a hedge fund billionaire or if you want to work at a really elite law firm, where you go to college can make some difference. It also impresses people when they learn that you attended a top college, and it can help in getting your first job. But the truly crazy idea is that one *has* to go to a selective school or that one *has* to be a top student in order to create a meaningful life. Yet this is the message kids get from parents, school, colleges, and even other kids, who infect each other with this kind of delusional thinking. Did you know that Jeff Bezos is the only CEO of the nation's top ten corporations with an Ivy League degree? And only eleven CEOs in the top one hundred were Ivy Leaguers. So if being a Big Boss is your kid's dream, they will be in good company even if they go to State U. Or, consider that only 0.8 percent of college students attend the country's top twelve colleges, yet quite a few more than 0.8 percent of college graduates go on to develop successful, meaningful, and fulfilled lives.

It worries us greatly when we see kids attach their identity to a grade, or a college acceptance letter, thinking that these things will inevitably make them happy. In the late summer of 2023, Bill, some educators, and a physician who studies student stress met with a group of middle and high school students in a high-achieving school district in Ohio. He and the other adults were stunned by the clarity with which the students communicated, "I am my grades." They all agreed that the most important thing in their life was getting into a good college. Bill asked, "Did anyone ever tell you that if you don't do well in high school, you can get thirty credits from a community college and then apply to most of the colleges in this country without showing your high school transcript?" Most of the kids rolled their eyes, and one kid said, speaking for the rest, "We'd never go to a community college."

You might be thinking this too—that you don't want your kid going to community college, or that college prestige gives you an outsized advantage. But consider this: You already know that Bill graduated from college with a 2.8 GPA (rounding up), flunked out of graduate school the first time he went, and was fired from his first job as a neuropsychologist. Ned withdrew from college and worked in restaurants for a year. Most of Ned's peers went on to jobs in finance after graduation, but Ned had no clue what to do. He picked up a newspaper and saw a classified ad looking for people who were "good at standardized tests and like working with high school kids." He got a job with the test-prep group and made a paltry salary working seven days a week for ten months of the year. People he met constantly asked him, "So what's your other job?" Long story short: Ned owns a test-prep company with offices in two states and the District of Columbia that's been around for twenty-five years and has helped thousands of kids.

Also, between the two of us, we know dozens, or more likely hundreds, of people who were late bloomers, "failed their way" to successful lives, and are happy and fulfilled even though they weren't excellent students, didn't get a college degree, or don't make a ton of money. We also know dozens, if not hundreds, of people who have achieved great career and financial success but are woefully lacking anything that resembles peace and happiness. A high-status education doesn't guarantee happiness, even for people in high-status professions. For instance, a study of lawyers found that factors like autonomy, a sense of relatedness, and intrinsic motivation were much more highly correlated with happiness than income, class rank, or making law review, which ranged from low to zero. Or consider the disturbing statistic that physicians experience depression and commit suicide at a far greater rate than the general population; for male physicians, the suicide rate is 40 percent higher, and for female physicians, it's 130 percent higher. We're not saying, "Stay clear of med school!" but we are saying that the stresses and sleep deprivation associated with getting into and getting through medical school and residency can change the developing brain in a way that lowers the chance that physicians will be able to enjoy their success. In our view, the most important outcome of childhood and adolescence isn't where a kid goes to college—it is the health of the brain kids will carry into adulthood.

Below we've listed some research-backed statements about what an accurate model of reality looks like:

Where you go to college really doesn't matter that much. (It matters much more what you do when you're there.)

Good relationships keep us healthier, and they keep us happier.

Money matters, but not nearly as much as we think it does.

People succeed by devoting themselves to what they care about and what they're good at, not one or the other.

We're actually not very good at predicting what will make us happy.

Accomplishments matter, but only as a measurement of your sense of competency.

Being happy—not "successful"—is an outsized determinant of good health.

We're happier when we give things to others than when we get things for ourselves.

If we're on a bus or plane, we're happier if we talk to a stranger than if we keep to ourselves.

The pleasure or "rush" we get from achieving things we want doesn't produce lasting happiness.

Some of these statements might sound familiar to you. They come from experts who have published books about their research, like Sonja Lyubomirsky (*The Myths of Happiness*) and Daniel Gilbert (*Stumbling on Happiness*). You might have heard one of them on a podcast or seen a Netflix special, or had a friend repeat their favorite nugget after *they* read one of the books or listened to a podcast. There is a small army of people out there encouraging us to wake up, unplug, and reconnect. But do we hear them, really? Here are three important questions to think about. Be honest with yourself—we won't tell.

▶ How many of the statements do you give lip service to without actually believing? For example, you might say to your kid, "It doesn't matter where you go to college," but, in the middle of the night, are you googling entrance requirements to Penn?

_____

_____

_____

▶ For how many of these do you think, "Yeah, but . . ." and think of all the counterarguments you'd make?

_____

_____

_____

▶ How many of these do you sincerely believe, but then catch yourself living, or parenting, in a way that negates it?

_____

_____

_____

Happiness or Pleasure?

In *What Do You Say?* we explained the differences between pleasure and happiness, and the different neurochemistry that supports each of them. Pleasure is about short-term gratification, and, by the way, gratification is fantastic. We don't want to take pleasure away from anyone. Pleasure, including the pleasure from drinking good wine, from a great experience, or from an important accomplishment, involves the neurotransmitter dopamine. But the problem with dopamine is that it doesn't last long. Dopamine levels reset very quickly, and the pleasure you get from these things is fleeting.

> Relationships contribute much more to happiness than academic, career, or financial accomplishment.

Also, too much pleasure-induced dopamine reduces serotonin, which is the neurotransmitter most associated with contentment and long-lasting happiness. If you have too little serotonin/contentment, then you seek more and more dopamine/pleasure, which stifles serotonin, and on and on and on it goes. You can get locked in an addictive cycle. We have seen this again and again with highly stressed kids at high-achieving schools, who drink to excess or use drugs to get that dopamine high because their serotonin is so low that they need *something* to keep them from falling off a cliff. They seek pleasure to offset their lack of happiness, which is probably why students at high-achieving schools are at much higher risk for substance use disorders than the general population from adolescence through at least their mid twenties.

Unlike pleasure, real happiness isn't fleeting. It's not that happy people don't grieve when they lose a loved one or feel less upbeat when they experience setbacks; it's that they are able to keep things in perspective and bounce back to their high baseline level of happiness before too long.

Below we've listed some happiness-inducing activities next to some that are pleasure-inducing, and left some blanks for you to fill in activities in your own life that contribute to your long-term happiness as opposed to activities that give you short-term pleasure. And again, pleasure isn't the bad guy here! But if you have a lot of pleasure and very little happiness, it's an imbalance worth looking at.

Pleasure is fleeting, happiness is lasting.

HAPPINESS/SEROTONIN	PLEASURE/DOPAMINE
Giving someone a gift they appreciate	Buying a coveted sweater
A moment of real connection with a good friend over a meal	A lot of Likes to your post on social media
Volunteering at a soup kitchen	Someone you like asking you out
Meditating	Getting high
Exercising outside	Getting good grades or academic honors
Doing work that feels meaningful	Getting a new car or video game
Donating money to a cause you believe in	Getting a raise or a promotion
Helping a neighbor who needs a hand	Winning a game
Joining a protest rally	Posting a protest statement on social media

Reflection question:

▶ When did something you thought would make you happy actually not make you very happy? Or maybe it did make you happy, but not for very long?

_____

_____

_____

During the period we were writing this book, Bill tested two similar high school seniors within the same month. Both boys were excellent students and outstanding athletes, and both were uncommonly (actually obsessively) driven to succeed. Both spent a good part of their high school years sleep-deprived and highly stressed, and, not surprisingly, both were on medication to reduce their anxiety and prevent depression. Both were accepted into highly elite colleges.

Bill saw one of the boys for testing a few weeks after his acceptance. During the clinical interview, Bill asked, "Are there times when you feel happy?" The boy answered, "I felt happy the day I got into college." Not the next day, or the day or week or month after that, but *the day* he got his acceptance email.

A few days later, Bill interviewed the other boy. His answer was exactly the same. Exactly. They both got into the colleges of their dreams, and their happiness lasted *one day.*

What makes us happy is so often not what we think will. Going to an elite college clearly is not a guaranteed ticket to happiness—the mental health crisis at highly elite schools is as worrisome, if not more worrisome, than at other schools. It would be great to learn these truths about happiness in high school, or in college, but for the most part kids don't. A class on happiness at Yale is the most popular course the university has ever offered, as students there are desperate to understand what really makes people happy (because getting into Yale didn't do it). This makes us wonder how many of those stressed and unhappy kids who take the course think, with frustrated exhaustion, "Why didn't someone tell me this sooner?"

A high-achieving friend of ours, Marnie, who works in sales, recently described how she closed two great deals in a single week. "It was such a rush," she said. She celebrated over the weekend and basked in the accomplishment of the recognition she'd earned. "And then the very next week," she said, "I had some things go wrong, and my progress on another project was slow, and I wondered if I'd ever sell anything else." She recognized she was being ridiculous, she said, but had a hard time generating the kind of energy she'd felt the week before.

We directed her to the work of Martin Seligman, who founded the field of positive psychology in the late 1990s. For true well-being, he has said, you need the following (known as PERMA):

Positive emotion

Engagement

Relationships

Meaning and purpose

Accomplishment

Marnie was focused on accomplishment, which, while part of the formula, is just one of five components. If she wasn't accomplishing, she felt listless. She needed to redirect her attention, and to give appreciation to the incredible relationships she had in her life—including with a friend in crisis who she'd been able to help during the "bad sales week." Or the way that she'd volunteered a good portion of her time over the previous weekend working at a community goodwill event, which aligned with her values and gave her a great sense of meaning. Accomplishment would not bring her sustainable happiness—it was just a piece of a much larger puzzle, and she wasn't attending to the whole thing.

We each have our own "bad sales weeks" when we need to realign our brains back to a state of contentedness. Bill tends to get the most distressed when he thinks a client is upset with him or that he's let someone down. But he knows that, while there are some genetically imposed limits to it, positive emotion contributes significantly to happiness, and that there are concrete things he can do to increase it: Regular and consistent sleep, exercise, meditation, and yoga are his go-tos. He also "talks back" to the three kinds of distorted thinking that create the most emotional distress, including (1) *should*-ing, or thinking, *This shouldn't be happening because the world should be different* (as if Bill has seen the plan for how the universe should be), (2) blowing things out of proportion (*This is a disaster*), and (3) predicting a negative future (*Maybe this will hurt my practice*).

Ned tends to feel the worst when he perceives social rejection. In these instances, he returns to PERMA, and focuses on the sense of meaning and purpose he gets from his job tutoring kids. There's always another kid to help, and he knows that doing so also helps *him* regain solid ground. He also challenges his negative emotions, and ensures that getting good sleep, exercising, and meditating take priority.

Exercise: Your Personal PERMA

Now it's your turn to look at the five elements of PERMA.

Under what circumstances do you feel the following?

Positive emotion (this could be something like watching a funny show, attending a family dinner or reunion, exercising, meditating, or interacting with a child or an animal):

_____

_____

_____

Engagement (this is akin to a feeling of flow, or being "in the zone," where you are completely caught up in whatever it is you're focused on):

_____

_____

_____

Relationships (this might be a long lunch with a friend where you're really focusing on them and feel connected to them):

_____

_____

_____

Meaning and purpose (this could be community service or attending a religious service, but it could also be raising your children, walking your dog, the content of your job, political involvement, or bringing food to a neighbor):

_____

_____

_____

Accomplishment (this is the good grade in school, or closing the deal, or earning an accolade):

_____

_____

_____

Where does your energy most often go? Make a pie chart with percentages showing how much you emphasize each.

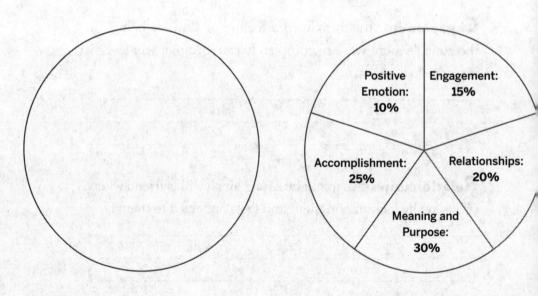

When you're feeling blue, is one of the five elements of PERMA getting short shrift? Which one?

_____

_____

_____

_____

These questions may seem irrelevant to parenting, but we assure you, they're actually central. If parents say—as most do—that what they want most for their kids is for them to be happy, then parents need to understand what happiness is made of, teach that to their kids, and model it as best they can. For instance, we *know* that healthy relationships really matter for happiness. How much time do you spend talking about your kids' relationships and how important they are compared to the time you spend talking about their homework, grades, activities, performance in sports and other extracurriculars, and chores?

Now it's your child's turn. You can fill in what *you* think they'd answer, or, if they're willing, have them fill it in themselves.

Under what circumstances do you feel the following?

Positive emotion (this could be something like watching a funny show, eating your favorite meal, getting exactly what you wanted for your birthday, or playing with your dog or cat):

_____

_____

_____

Engagement (this is akin to a feeling of flow, where you are completely caught up in whatever it is you're focused on):

_____

_____

_____

Relationships (talking to a friend who cares about you and doesn't judge you, or feeling happy being with your extended family):

_____

_____

_____

Meaning and purpose (this could be community service, but it could also be helping at home, walking your dog, making a teacher smile, or bringing food to a neighbor):

_____

_____

_____

Accomplishment (this is the good grade in school, the tournament win, or earning an accolade):

_____

_____

_____

Where does their/your energy most often go? Fill in this pie chart with percentages showing how much they/you emphasize each.

When they're/you're feeling down, is one of the five elements of PERMA getting short shrift? Which one?

_____

_____

_____

Would they like your help accessing an element of PERMA?

_____

_____

_____

Choosing a Life That Fits You

Recently, a mom reached out to thank us for our advice to let her son make his own decisions and find his own way. Now a young man in his thirties, her son is *happy*. He works as a rock musician, and makes extra money by doing part-time service jobs. His mom said that while it's not exactly the kind of life *she* would have chosen for him, she wouldn't change any of the choices he made along the way, as it was these choices (and not what she thought would be best for him) that enabled him to feel happy and fulfilled. With so many of the young adults she sees around her feeling anxious, lonely, and unhappy, her son's happiness is not something she takes for granted. He recently got engaged, and his fiancée remarked to his mother that he is uncommonly self-assured, which she said was because he completely trusts his own decisions. His mom attributes that quality to all the practice he had in learning from his choices as a teenager and young adult. He knows what he needs to be happy, and he pursues it.

Part of our job as parents is to help kids create the life they want. When they're teenagers, help them identify what they love to do and what they can do better than most people, which can get them thinking about how they can contribute to the world. This inevitably means recognizing that they're not going to be good at everything, and that's the way it should be. We want to normalize the idea that we all have shortcomings; that's fine, and even necessary, as the world functions best when its populace has a diverse skill set. There are so many ways to contribute in this world, and they don't always require making a lot of money or being at the top of one's field.

> You become successful by working really hard at something you enjoy and that comes easily to you.

Questions for your kids:

What do you think you do better than a lot of people?

What do you love to spend time doing?

When do you feel most alive?

Which friends do you feel closest to?

Which friends are you most able to be yourself with?

When have you felt you've really contributed to something?

What are the most important things in your life?

If there's a reason you're on this planet, what do you think it might be?

Is there anything you'd like to change about your life?

Keep using these questions—they shouldn't be asked once and then discarded. Put them up on your refrigerator or bulletin board.

Reflection questions:

▶ When you were young, what messages did you get from adults about what it takes to be happy in adulthood?

_____

_____

_____

▶ Now that you're the adult, you get to answer: What do you think it takes to be happy in adulthood? Were the messages you received right?

_____

_____

_____

▶ When have you personally felt really happy?

_____

_____

_____

▶ What messages do you think you're giving your child about what it takes to be happy in adulthood?

_____

_____

_____

▶ Is there a discrepancy between what you've tried to communicate about happiness and what your kid thinks about happiness?

_____

_____

_____

▶ Do you see any patterns across the generations about conceptions of happiness?

_____

_____

_____

Now, go back to the rating system at the top of the chapter.

Is there anything you'd rate differently now?

_____

_____

_____

Are there any that you send mixed messages about?

_____

_____

_____

Do you spend time in conversation with your child about the things you've rated most highly? What about the ones you don't? Does the distribution of time and energy given to each make sense?

_____

_____

_____

Would you feel comfortable *sharing* your answers with your child? Why or why not?

_____

_____

_____

 **Cross-Check:**

Principle 1—*Put Connection First*

Principle 6—*Be a Nonanxious Presence in Your Family*

Motivate Your Kids Without Trying to Change Them

Most parents want to change their kids in some way. Parents want their kids to be more motivated for school, to work harder at sports, to go to church, to be more respectful to grandma, to stop leaving the towel on the bathroom floor, to spend less time on video games or social media, to be less anxious, to be more cooperative and not need to be told ten times, or to stop hanging around with kids who are bad influences. But the thing is, you cannot change someone else. You can try to help them change, but if they don't want your help, you'll get conflict and resistance every time. This is both one of the clearest truths in life and yet one of the hardest to absorb, as evidenced by the fact that parents ask us every week how they can change their child. "How can I get my son to be more motivated in school?" "How can I convince my daughter that ghosts aren't real?" "How can I make them exercise more?" "How can I get her to see that social media is ruining her life?" And, most starkly, "How can I get my child to stop using drugs?" They often explain that they've "tried everything," which usually includes encouraging, lecturing, scolding, threatening, rewarding, withdrawing privileges, taking away their phone or video games, and bribing—without success.

When someone we love behaves in a way that we don't like and that we perceive isn't good for them, it's painful. It's hard to grasp that we can't convince them to change—or use our energy to force them to change. There are logical reasons they should alter their behavior, after all: "I just need to use reason with them, and if I tell them enough times, they'll wake up and want to change!" And yet, they don't and won't change unless *they find their own reasons to*.

This isn't to say that people can't change. They can and they do all the time. And it also isn't to say that there's nothing you can do—there's actually a lot. But the focus needs to be on what *you* do, rather than on how to change someone else. The first step? Acknowledging this truth.

What would you like to see your kid do differently? If you could change one thing about your kid, what would it be?

_____

_____

_____

What have you done in the past to try to get your kid to change? What was effective and what wasn't?

_____

_____

_____

What did your parents try to change about you?

_____

_____

_____

Your answers to the above questions might vary dramatically, but the common experience is that if we set out to change someone, it usually doesn't go well unless they're asking you to help them change. Our attempts to change a person often put distance between us and the person we'd like to see change. Kids frequently tell us things like, "When my parents get on me about working harder in school, I feel even less motivated to get started on my assignments."

▶ When you think about giving up on the idea that you can change your kids, does it feel liberating or threatening? If it feels threatening, how so? Do your objections seem rational?

_____

_____

_____

▶ What are you afraid would happen if you didn't try to change your child?

_____

_____

_____

Now, try to remember a time when someone tried to get you to change. Maybe it was a friend trying to get you to see your way out of a bad relationship. Maybe it was a parent trying to get you to eat more healthfully or to look for a part-time job. Maybe it was your partner trying to get you to manage your anger better, to spend less money shopping, to play less golf, or to stop yelling at the kids.

Think back to the situation or situations.

▶ What was said or done? What was communicated to you, and how did it make you feel?

_____

_____

_____

▶ How did you respond? Did it work in the short term? Did you change your actions?

_____

_____

_____

▶ Did it work in the long term? Did you change as a person?

_____

_____

_____

▶ Did the person's attempt to get you to change impact your relationship with them?

_____

_____

_____

▶ What has prompted you to make changes in your own life?

_____

_____

_____

To try to motivate someone is to try to change them.

"I just wish Samantha worked harder in school," a dad told us plaintively. "She loves reading manga, chatting online with other manga fans, and writing her own fan fiction. She has plenty of time and energy for all of *that*. But school? Forget it. How can I motivate her?"

When a parent like this asks us how to motivate their child, they're really asking us how to *change* their child. Motivation and change are closely related, as no one changes without motivation to do so—and as no one becomes more motivated without changing. And so it follows that we can learn a lot about helping people change from the science of motivation—and vice versa.

Self-determination theory has been our North Star for many years, as it offers one of the most elegant and practical ways to think about helping others find the motivation to change. It holds that for children (and adults) to be internally motivated, three basic psychological needs must be met: a sense of relatedness, a sense of competence, and a sense of autonomy.

In our previous books we've told many stories of children, teens, and young adults who made significant changes in their lives when they experienced a stronger connection with a parent or teacher, felt more competent, or experienced a stronger sense of autonomy. When a teacher sees something wonderful in a kid and tells them so, it sets off a positive chain reaction. That kid feels competent in a way they hadn't before and works hard to please the teacher. And when a teacher or coach simply shows interest in a student, such as by asking about their life outside of school or soccer, and treats them respectfully, the strong sense of relatedness that results can fuel a kid's motivation to do well. Dozens of studies show the power of supporting students' autonomy for increasing their motivation. On the flip side, we've seen hundreds of kids who experienced other people's attempts to change them as weakening their relationship with the person who is trying to "control" them, as making them feel less competent, and as making them feel that they're being coerced. So if our kids are struggling, instead of clamping down and trying to manage every part of their lives, what will actually help is if we focus on maintaining—or even deepening—our connection with them, as they are, on helping them experience themselves as competent, and on supporting their autonomy.

▶ Have you had the experience of working harder for a parent, a teacher, or a boss with whom you have a good relationship than you would have otherwise?

_____

_____

_____

▶ Can you think of a time when someone made you feel more competent? How did that affect your motivation?

_____

_____

_____

▶ How about a time someone conveyed confidence in your ability to handle things on your own?

_____

_____

_____

▶ Now, think about who seems to have the most success motivating your child. Who does your child seem to listen to the most? Who seems to have the most influence on them? What do you think it is about this person that motivates your kid to think or behave differently?

_____

_____

_____

▶ Have your kids ever changed in ways that surprised you, in response to something that happened that was unexpected?

_____

_____

_____

▶ Between relatedness, competence, and autonomy, which do you emphasize most with your kids? What do you do to promote each?

_____

_____

_____

▶ Think about positive changes in your child's habits or behavior that you didn't cause. Why do you think they changed?

_____

_____

_____

Bringing it back to Samantha's dad, we suggested that he start with empathy rather than judgment. We advised him to say something like, "I know how much you love manga, and I can see why. The stories are exciting and the illustrations are incredible, and I see how much fun you have communicating with other manga nuts. I've also been impressed by how hard you work on your fan fiction, and I see that you're becoming a really good writer. I understand and respect that school currently isn't your highest priority, and I'm not going to try to change that. At the same time, if it's okay with you, I'd like to share some of my thoughts about why school may be more important for what you want to do than you currently think it is. You can do what you want with what I say—I know that you can make a good decision for yourself." Relatedness, competence, and autonomy are baked into that simple statement. What Samantha's dad wants is influence, not power. And he can best earn it by treating Samantha respectfully and by helping her find her own motivation to do things differently.

We advised Samantha's dad to support her interest in manga (rather than try to talk her out of it) because kids' intrinsic motivation appears to develop through what social scientist Reed Larson calls "the passionate pursuit of pastimes." As Larson explains, when kids do things that they're passionate about, they enter a state of "flow" or complete engagement, which involves full attention and present-centeredness, high effort and determination, and low stress. It's the kind of brain state we want to be in much of the time in our adult life.

The importance of this "passionate pursuit of pastimes" isn't obvious to most parents, so one of the most common impulses we have when our kids aren't working as hard at something as we think they *should* is to take away things they *want* to do. The problem with this approach is that, in our experience, it's never once motivated a kid to work harder. It might make her life miserable enough that she complies, but that's not intrinsic motivation. It might not seem to make sense to let Samantha spend time on manga if her grades are suffering, but it actually makes complete sense. Her engagement in manga fosters the development of the intrinsic motivation circuits in the brain such that she's able to work really hard at things she thinks are important. (Since she loves to write, it's likely that school will eventually become more important to Samantha, by which time she'll have trained her brain to work really hard at it.) In a time when kids so rarely engage deeply, the passionate pursuit of pastimes may be the one opportunity for them to wire a brain capable of deeper engagement.

Exercise: Flow Audit

How much time does your child spend working hard on challenging tasks or activities they love and that are important to them?

_____

_____

_____

How much time does your child spend on tasks or activities in order to earn a grade, to receive a reward, or to avoid punishment?

_____

_____

_____

Talk with your kids and tell them you want to make sure there's enough time in their day for what they love to do. How can you help them find and protect this time?

_____

_____

_____

Caveat

Importantly, if what your child loves to do is play video games, scroll TikTok or other social media, or watch television or YouTube videos, these probably don't count as big builders of intrinsic motivation. Watching TikTok and television are passive pursuits that don't require the kind of effort and determination needed to write a good story, climb a wall, improve your jump shot, or nail a guitar solo by listening to it over and over. And video games don't really require self-motivation—because psychologists, behavioral engineers, and programmers design these games by using motivational techniques that will make them as addictive as possible. Because of the way the games are designed, it's much harder to stop playing than it is to keep going. It's not that you should forbid these activities; they're fine for entertainment if kids are old enough. But they aren't the kind of passions that help shape a motivated brain.

When you're frustrated by your child's lack of motivation for something you think is important, notice if you have the impulse to take something away from them. Have you done this in the past? Has it worked, beyond getting them to comply short-term? Did it work even for that? How did it affect your relationship?

_____

_____

_____

_____

_____

_____

_____

_____

_____

Helping Kids Find Their Own Reasons to Change

As we covered in our book *What Do You Say?*, most of us are ambivalent about making a change in our lives. You might actually want to change. Perhaps you genuinely want to exercise more or to drink less coffee. But each of these things requires work, or sacrifice, or has a downside you're not terribly excited about. If your partner says, "You're drinking another cup of coffee? Don't you think you should take it easy? It makes you so jittery when you drink too much," you might say, "Yeah, I know," but some part of you is also likely to get defensive. *I like coffee! Geez, it's not like it's crack. As far as vices go, it's not such a big deal.* But if your partner says, "I know you love your coffee, even though it makes you jittery. And it's so cold and dark here in the winter, it's hard to think about cutting back," are you not then more apt to wonder if you could have just a *little* less? Because you do really hate that jittery feeling you get when you've had too much.

This isn't trickery or manipulation, by the way. Your partner isn't telling you something they disagree with, they're just expressing empathy and validating one side of your ambivalence. Because you want to feel good, of course you know you shouldn't consume so much coffee. But you also know cutting back isn't easy.

We created the chart below to help you peek inside a kid's mixed feelings on a variety of common issues:

ON THE ONE HAND, THEY'RE THINKING (AND OFTEN VERBALIZING) *THIS* . . .	BUT THEY'RE ALSO THINKING *THIS* . . .
I hate doing homework. It's boring and confusing, and sometimes it makes me feel stupid.	I really want to get good grades, and when I just get started on my homework it tends to go okay.
I don't want to stop hanging out with Chelsea. She's fun and interesting and popular.	Chelsea can be kind of mean sometimes, and I don't feel great about myself when I'm with her.
I don't want to go to bed so early because nighttime is the only time I have for myself, without anyone telling me what to do.	I've been pretty tired lately and know that if I don't get to bed, I'll be grumpy in the morning and the day won't start out well.
I don't want breakfast in the morning. I'm not hungry when I first wake up, and if I skip breakfast, I can sleep for ten more minutes.	When I don't have breakfast, I get hungry in second period and have a hard time concentrating.
I don't want to join the debate team. I'll get embarrassed if I mess up, and I don't want the stress of it all.	I've been told by a few adults that I'm a good debater, and my best friend is joining the team. It would be cool to see if I'm really good at it.

Holding ambivalent feelings is pretty tiring, if you think about it. And the more someone presses on one side of the ambivalence scale, the more you are likely to argue the other side, just to keep things in some sort of equilibrium.

If your child expresses the feelings in the left-hand side of the column, chances are decent that you respond with arguments from the right-hand side. But when you do this, your kid may double down on the left-hand side.

Which leads to our next exercise:

What do you think your child might be feeling ambivalent about? Don't let their outward certainty fool you. Samantha, for instance, might swear up and down that she doesn't spend too much time on manga, when in reality she might be concerned about how her school performance is suffering.

What are the arguments they've made—or that you can imagine them making—on either side? Fill in the chart below.

ON THE ONE HAND . . .	ON THE OTHER HAND . . .

What if, instead of arguing the right-hand side, you instead validated the left-hand side? Does the conversation change?

_____

_____

_____

Understanding ambivalence is a key component of another of our favorite approaches to motivation: motivational interviewing. When we were working on *What Do You Say?*, we talked with a high school counselor who used motivational interviewing to help a student cut back on her pot smoking—and eventually give it up altogether—without explicitly doing anything to try to get her to limit her pot use. The counselor did it by talking to the student respectfully, asking her questions and reflecting back what she understood the girl to be saying, and looking for "change talk"—or the girl's voicing her own reasons for changing. Shortly after we spoke to the counselor, Bill tested Blake, a fifteen-year-old boy who had just finished his ninth-grade year. He was struggling a bit in school, but he was a very good basketball player and was highly motivated to make his school's varsity team as a tenth grader. In Bill's first meeting with Blake's parents, they talked about what sounded like attention-related problems and trouble with reading. They then mentioned their most significant concern, which was that their son seemed to be smoking pot every day. They reported that they lectured him and got rid of his stash when they first found him smoking, but that he just bought more and continued to use.

Because of the counselor's success with her student, and because of motivational interviewing's long history of success in helping problem drinkers, Bill sent Blake's parents a draft copy of the chapter in which this story was included, suggesting that they consider giving the same approach a try. So, a couple days later, when things were calm at home, Blake's mother opened up a conversation about his pot use by asking, without any judgment, "What do you like about pot? What does it do for you?" Blake then waxed rhapsodic about how much more mellow he feels when he smokes weed, how much more fun he has when he's with his friends, and how much less he worries about starting school again in the fall. His mother respectfully reflected back to Blake what she was hearing: "So pot makes you less anxious and makes it more fun to be with your friends—is that what you're saying?" Blake agreed, and he then went into more detail about the advantages of being high. After talking for a couple more minutes, however, he said to his mother, "But after I smoke, I can't push myself to practice as hard as I need to if I'm going to make varsity this year." His mom again simply reflected back what she heard Blake saying, and then asked, "Does that feel like a big problem?" Blake said that it did. He'd found his own reason to change. His mom then asked, "Any ideas about what to do with this situation?" Blake answered that maybe he should cut back, and by the end of the summer he was no longer smoking.

This approach won't work every time, and if kids seem to have prolonged substance use, we recommend seeking professional help. But it illustrates the idea that parents have a lot of power to help their kids change in positive ways without explicitly *trying* to change them. Blake's mom later acknowledged that this motivational interviewing approach felt scary to her because it could sound to Blake like she was endorsing his pot use if she listened respectfully and didn't (1) clearly criticize him, (2) tell him he needed to stop, and (3) let him know what the consequences would be if he didn't. But she also said that it felt freeing because she had so often used lecturing, scolding, nagging, and threatening to try to get Blake to change, which never worked, and which just put more tension in her relationship with her son.

From a self-determination theory perspective, respectful listening and not rushing to tell Blake what he needed to do helped him feel closer to his mom—and increased their relatedness. Also, by asking if pot use was something he'd like to change, she promoted his sense of competence ("I trust that you can figure this out"), as well as his sense of autonomy.

Exercise: Questioning Change

Ask your kid: "Are there things you'd like to change about your life?"

If there are, and if the variables are within their control (being taller or getting his divorced parents back together again wouldn't count), ask, "What have you tried so far to make a change?"

Then ask, "Is this something you'd like help with? If so, how can I help?"

You can change, yourself.

We came to realize years ago that when our kids are not doing well, our most important work is often on ourselves. This commonly means managing our own worry, fear, anger, guilt, or tendency to catastrophize—and resisting things that make problems worse. One analogy we use here is ballroom dancing. In ballroom, you can't change your partner's steps, but you can change yours, and that impacts the way you move together. Families are the same. If parents change their steps, the kids likely will too.

What steps can you change? For one, you can change the energy. As we've already covered, parents often work harder to get their kid to do better than their kid does, which never goes well. The time-honored tools of lecturing repeatedly, scolding, sharing advice whether it's wanted or not, and threatening at least make parents feel like they're doing *something*, and they don't have to experience the stress and dread that comes from feeling helpless. But the fights that ensue are never helpful, and fighting about the same thing over and over is always toxic. The good news is that it takes two to fight, and if you decide not to, you've taken a powerful step. By deciding that you are not going to fight, you can use your energy more wisely and skillfully.

For another, you can change the behaviors you're willing to accommodate and the pursuits you're willing to support financially. Consider failure-to-launch young adults. We've noticed parents almost invariably spend their energy ineffectively trying to motivate or manipulate them to take classes or do volunteer work, or simply telling them that they need to do *something* productive. But when the focus is on what we want the young adult to change, we're in a powerless position; we can't *make* them get off the couch and get out of the house. It's much more effective when parents focus on what *they* do or, more specifically, on what they are willing or not willing to do for their adult child—and what they can and cannot support. When parents focus on maintaining a close relationship with their adult child but are not willing to provide spending money or to pay for things the young person should be paying for, it's more effective than lecturing, scolding, threatening, or shaming. The same principle is true at younger ages. If your sixth grader is perpetually forgetful (soccer cleats, lunch, homework), you don't have to interrupt your workday to bring whatever they've left at home to them. If you've had tension with your preteen about their tendency to binge shows on Netflix, there's no rule that says you have to pay for the subscription.

Bill recently worked with a high school boy with autism and ADHD who is bright enough to go to college and says that he wants to. However, his parents told Bill that they are running the college search and admissions process—not their son, who only takes the steps required to get into college when they're "right on top of him." As we mentioned in Principle 2, if a young person isn't ready to run this process himself, he's not ready for college.

Bill advised the parents to change the energy by not working harder than their son to make college happen. They could also focus on where they have leverage, which, in this case, is in the financial domain. Bill suggested that the parents tell their son they feel fine about spending a small fortune on a college education for him—but they first want to be sure he's ready to go. Bill recommended that they then talk with their son about the kinds of things they need to see in order to know that he's ready—like getting himself into and out of bed independently, doing more than the bare minimum on school assignments, keeping up with his reading load, managing his time well, and asking for help when he needs it. Once this is on the table, it's on the boy to show his parents that he's ready for college—rather than on the parents to try to make it happen for him.

If it feels like you're working harder to help your kid than he is, change the energy.

Change Comes When They're Ready

Our friend James and his wife worried for years about their daughter Maya, who was shy and anxious as a young child and seemed to be growing more anxious by the day. She frequently asked her parents to reassure her, and she avoided new situations and friendships. When James asked us for advice, we told him to ask Maya, "Is this something you would like to be different?" Maya said no.

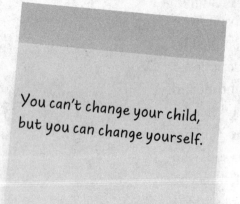

You can't change your child, but you can change yourself.

When kids come to a place where their anxiety is impacting their life enough, they tend to be more open to the possibility of change. Maya was not ready to change. She knew change would be hard work because it would require her to face her fears, and she had no interest in doing that.

A few years passed, during which time Maya's parents tried different interventions with her. First they bought an anti-anxiety workbook to go through with Maya, and offered her incentives for every chapter she finished. She went through the motions of reading and answering questions, but she wasn't interested in changing, so it didn't do any good at all. They used bribery to get her to try meditation. They bought her stress balls and lavender oil and all of the things they could think of, but nothing seemed to cut through her resistance to confronting her anxiety. During this time, whenever they asked her, "Maya, is this something you would like to be different?" she continued to say no. When her teacher commented that her anxiety was getting in the way of her ability to focus in class, her parents did what a lot of parents do when their kid is struggling: They clamped down tighter. They insisted she see a therapist "just for a few sessions." Maya had little choice but to go along with it. But she didn't seem to benefit from the therapy in any way, and she protested before each appointment, so her parents let it go.

A year later, when she was twelve, Maya's anxiety grew much worse. She was fearful and unhappy most of the time. She was struggling with schoolwork, with her friendships, and with her health. She was fighting with her parents and her siblings much more than ever before. Her parents asked her, again: "Maya, is this something you would like to be different?"

This time she said yes.

They sprang into action and were able to find her a therapist. Maya's improvement did not happen overnight, but within six months she was a much different kid. She finally *wanted* to change, and that made all the difference.

It might seem like Maya's parents were helpless, but actually there's a lot that they did in the time before Maya was ready to deal with her anxiety. They changed their own steps in the dance. For instance, one of Maya's dance steps was to refuse to go to social events with her family. School potlucks, neighborhood parties, and even extended family holidays caused Maya a lot of anxiety, so one of her parents had always stayed home with her while everyone else in the family went. Maya's parents could not make her want to be less anxious or change her in any way. But they did stop making accommodations to try to prevent her from feeling anxious. They expressed confidence in her ability to handle her anxiety, and they were clear about what they were willing to do for her, and what they were not. They

Two of the most powerful questions you can ask your child are "Is this something you'd like to be different?" and "Is there a way that I can help?"

told Maya they were not willing to miss out on social events. Maya could wait in the car or outside if she wouldn't go in, but her parents would no longer stay home with her.

Reflection questions:

Think about a situation in which you and your child are at an impasse.

▶ What can you do to change your steps in the dance?

_____

_____

_____

▶ Can you stick to that change, even if faced with resistance? How will you be able to do that?

_____

_____

_____

▶ Are you trying to change you? Or are you trying to change your kid?

_____

_____

_____

 **Cross-Check:**

Principle 1—_Put Connection First_

Principle 2—_Be a Consultant, Not a Boss or Manager_

Principle 6—_Be a Nonanxious Presence in Your Family_

6

Be a Nonanxious Presence in Your Family

It's report card day. The moment grades are due to be posted, your high school junior logs on to the school server. He's been worried for days about whether those last few assignments he turned in to get his grades up did the job. While some of his friends make a big show of not caring about their grades, a far greater percentage of them do. He knows that the group chats that night and conversations the next day at school will be about how everyone did, and what it might mean for college admissions. For your part, you're nervous too. He's such a good kid but he wasn't focused this term. You worry that you should have pushed him more, that he's going to be demoralized, and that doors will be closed to possible futures. *I mean, all the parent groups talk about is how hard it is to get into a good college.* Your stomach flip-flops while you wait. When your son looks up from the computer, his expression tells the whole story. Whatever he saw on that screen wasn't good.

How do you respond?

A) You go into crisis-management mode and suggest that the two of you create a plan to mitigate the damage.

B) You tell him it will be fine, that he'll still have good college choices even with a bad grade in an important year.

C) You work hard to hide your own fear and suggest that you go out for pizza or watch a show to get his mind off his troubles.

D) You give in to getting mad, and you show it. If he hadn't slacked off so much, he wouldn't be in this position. He needs to understand that his work ethic is a problem, and while you hate to pile on while he's down, he needs to hear tough messages sometimes.

E) You ask if he wants to talk about it, and if he says yes, you listen. If he says no, you let him be, but tell him you love him no matter what, and that you're one-hundred-percent confident he can handle whatever comes his way.

Reflection questions:

▶ Which of these responses makes the most sense to you?

_____

_____

_____

▶ Which are you most likely to do in the moment?

_____

_____

_____

▶ How has responding in this way worked for you in the past?

_____

_____

_____

▶ Which most aligns with your values?

_____

_____

_____

▶ Which is most like how you would have wanted your parents to have reacted in a similar situation?

_____

_____

_____

▶ How do you think your kid would react to each?

_____

_____

_____

Option A is pretty tempting. As mammals, we're wired to protect and soothe our young. So it's only natural that we want to come to the rescue! When we feel like we don't have control of a situation, it feels good to *take* control. But the problem with this response is that it reveals that you're pretty worried about this whole grades situation too. And what's more, that you don't really trust your son to handle it without you. It *seems* like you're helping, but you might actually be increasing his anxiety and undermining his sense that he's got this.

Option B also seems reasonable. You're attempting to soothe your kid's hard feelings by sharing another point of view. You don't want him to dwell on the report card, and you don't want him to pick up on your own feelings of distress. But there are a couple of problems with Option B: As much as we'd like to, we can't really hide our anxious feelings from our kids—it's as if they have special sensors and pick up on them despite our best efforts. Those anxious feelings spread much like a virus does, and the more we try to cover them up, the more they think, *Oh crap, it must be really bad. I must have really screwed up my life.* This option also denies them the opportunity to process their emotions of stress, disappointment, and fear—and those emotions are going to have to come out one way or another. Another problem with B: It reinforces the idea that successful lives are about avoiding difficulties and natural consequences, and signals that, as a parent, you may not be up to hanging out with the hard feelings that so often accompany messy situations. One more thing: The more we try to talk kids out of their hard feelings, the tighter they hold on to them.

Option C is attractive—or at least instinctive—to a lot of parents, and may be the most common response, even if they sense that those know-it-alls who write parenting books wouldn't approve. Yet remember from Principle 3 how kids feel pressure to excel, whether or not parents think they're signaling it. Kids quite naturally don't want to disappoint their parents. And while certainly some anxiety is healthy and propels us to do smart things like being aware of our surroundings in isolated parking lots, what's much more common is that anxiety causes our amygdala to take over any hope of our prefrontal cortex getting a say. Put another way, your son is already anxious about disappointing you. Add that to his anxiety about the future, and what he rightly sees as *your* anxiety about his future, and any chance for him to be clearheaded about how to move forward is out the window. It's also true that, while we don't want to shield kids from natural consequences, when we don't show empathy—and instead fall into wielding teachable moments like an "I told you so" cudgel—kids are likely to turn their hard feelings *on us*, ginning up reasons to be mad at or blame us. Option C is therefore unlikely to be effective and is much more apt to drive a wedge between you and your kid at the time that he most needs some support. The plain truth is that trying to teach a lesson or impart wisdom if you're mad or highly anxious (and, by definition, can't think straight) won't bring the result you want.

The likelihood of your kid hearing your message if you're mad is close to zero.

Bottom line: We don't want to be the cause of our kids' anxiety. And there's no better way to prevent that from happening than by meeting disappointment, fear, and worry with calm, compassion, and confidence. As you probably surmised, then, **Option D** is the answer we'd go with.

Every experienced parent knows that it's much easier to soothe an infant if we stay calm, to help a distressed young child if we can stay calm, and to help an angry teenager if we can stay calm—and don't get stressed and angry ourselves. By developing our "calm button"—our ability to be what's called "a nonanxious presence"—we will have a much easier time communicating optimism to our kids. And the less anxious we

> When we're a nonanxious presence, we aren't emotionally overreactive, we're not burdened by excessive worry or fearfulness, and we communicate a courageous attitude toward life.

are, the easier it is to promote their sense of autonomy, which is a gift that keeps on giving throughout a lifetime. And it helps us teach them to face problems courageously—rather than fearfully.

But here's the thing about being a nonanxious presence: It's not easy. In fact, the Surgeon General issued an advisory on parental stress, which concludes that "41% of parents say most days they are so stressed they cannot function and 48% say that most days their stress is completely overwhelming compared to other adults (20% and 26%, respectively)." It isn't a sit-on-your-hands and zip-your-lip presence. It's an active presence that involves listening well, practicing empathy, not overreacting, and offering suggestions when they're welcomed. It's a *practice*—it's not something we read about once a week, and it's a lot easier if we have routines in our life for reducing our own stress and anxiety. The goal of this chapter is to help you develop your own nonanxious presence practice.

Understanding Emotional Contagion

Stress is contagious. Not only is the amygdala particularly skilled at picking up on stress from others, but the prefrontal cortex also has what are called mirror neurons, which allow us to observe and mimic the expressions of others. Mirror neurons are why we don't meet a friend's sadness or grief with smiles and giggles.

Several years ago, Ned was in a classroom taking the SAT along with thirty high schoolers. Test-prep tutors take the test regularly, to stay sharp on the kinds of questions that are on it, and more so to remind themselves of the experience of taking it. He noticed his pulse was incredibly elevated—140 beats per minute—which didn't make logical sense at first. Ned has taken the SAT dozens and dozens of times, is quite good at standardized tests, and had nothing to lose or gain from his test score. So why was he having an outsized stress response? Because he was in a small, airless room with thirty teenagers exuding stress hormones. Their tight body language, pained expressions, sweat, and smells all said, "Danger! This is a danger zone!"

Being a nonanxious presence isn't just about how you act but also about how you feel.

Contagion like this is important to understand for two reasons. First, because when you are anxious, mad, or worried, you are spreading it to those around you. Our children are born studying our facial cues, and even Cate Blanchett probably can't hide it from her offspring when she's worried. Second, when your child is stressed, anxious, or even just grumpy (as adolescents often are!), they are spreading their emotions to *you*. You are a dumpster for all the negative feelings, and you've got to empty it. Otherwise you and your family can enter a stress spiral together.

To fully grasp what stress contagion feels like, take a moment to answer this question:

Think about someone whose presence amps you up. What is it about them that is activating? Is it their voice? Their body language? Their words? Their facial expressions?

_____

_____

_____

In the past few years, amateur sports leagues have struggled to recruit enough referees because of the frequency with which they're verbally abused or physically attacked by parents. Some umpires and referees are even going to start wearing body cameras when doing games with ten- and eleven-year-old players! What do you imagine it's like for a child to see his parent out of control with anger over some trivial call?

_____

_____

_____

Contrast this with a child whose parent is a nonanxious presence: The good news is that calm is contagious too. You probably have someone in your life you turn to when you are looking to calm down or to feel reassured, even if this person isn't physically present with you.

So, now, as you think about this person whose presence is calming, what is it about them that gives this effect? How do they speak? What do they say? What do you think they believe about life that allows them to radiate calm?

_____

_____

_____

_____

_____

_____

_____

If you had to deal with something difficult, who would you turn to? What is their presence like? How would you want that person to respond to you?

_____

_____

_____

_____

_____

Our most important work as parents is usually on ourselves.

_____

_____

"Okay, But I'm Not Yoda. So, What Do I Do?"

A mother of two came up to us the other day looking irritated. "When you suggest I need to not just pretend, but actually *be* a calm presence amidst the storm, that just makes me feel *more* anxious. I'm a sensitive person, living with two adolescent girls, and their moods rub off on me. It's not like I can just not be me."

We agree! To expect that a parent is never going to feel anxious, stressed, fearful, or mad is unrealistic. But you can manage those feelings so that you can show up in a way that brings the temperature down for everyone. Remember that it's a process that starts with the decision *to move in the direction of* becoming a nonanxious presence. As you'll see, there's an in-the-moment component (calming or de-stressing yourself), which we compare to "emergency medicine," and a "preventative medicine" component that involves practices through which we can, over time, make our stress response less easily triggered, making it less likely that we will overreact when our kids aren't doing well.

STEP ONE: Assess your baseline stress level.

Remember that stress takes many forms. It can look like anxiety and avoidance (the "flight part" of the fight-or-flight response) or like anger and verbal or physical attack ("the fight part").

Take and score this test, the Perceived Stress Scale (PSS), to get an idea of your baseline stress level.

In the last month, how often have you . . .

1. Been upset because of something that happened unexpectedly?

    1. Never
    2. Almost never
    3. Sometimes
    4. Fairly often
    5. Very often

2. Felt that you were unable to control important things in your life?

    1. Never
    2. Almost never
    3. Sometimes
    4. Fairly often
    5. Very often

3. Felt nervous or stressed?

1. Never
2. Almost never
3. Sometimes
4. Fairly often
5. Very often

4. Felt confident about your ability to handle your personal problems?

1. Never
2. Almost never
3. Sometimes
4. Fairly often
5. Very often

5. Felt that things were going your way?

1. Never
2. Almost never
3. Sometimes
4. Fairly often
5. Very often

6. Found that you could not cope with all the things you had to do?

1. Never
2. Almost never
3. Sometimes
4. Fairly often
5. Very often

7. Been able to control irritations in your life?

1. Never
2. Almost never
3. Sometimes
4. Fairly often
5. Very often

8. Felt that you were on top of things?

1. Never
2. Almost never
3. Sometimes
4. Fairly often
5. Very often

9. Been angered because of things that happened that were out of your control?

1. Never
2. Almost never
3. Sometimes
4. Fairly often
5. Very often

10. Felt difficulties were piling up so high that you could not overcome them?

1. Never
2. Almost never
3. Sometimes
4. Fairly often
5. Very often

Scoring directions:

Reverse your scores for questions 4, 5, 7, and 8. On these four questions, change the scores like this:

1 = 5, 2 = 4, 3 = 3, 4 = 2, 5 = 1.

Now, add up your scores for each item to get a total. My total score is _____.

Scores can range from 10 to 50, with higher scores indicating higher perceived stress.

10–23: would be considered low stress

24–36: would be considered moderate stress

37–50: would be considered high perceived stress

STEP TWO: Identify your triggers. Under what circumstances does your anxiety level go up? It could be around places, like airports; activities, like driving or being in crowds; issues, like academics or housework; or physical symptoms, like hunger, fatigue, or nagging pain. It's helpful to know that most of us are triggered in situations that are unfamiliar or unpredictable, that feel threatening, and/or in which we feel we have very little control. Dr. Sonia Lupien, a neuroscientist at the Centre for Studies on Human Stress, has summarized these conditions with the acronym N.U.T.S. (because stress makes you nuts):

N = novelty; something new

U = unpredictability; no way of knowing what could occur

T = threat to your body or your ego; feeling your competence or integrity is in question

S = sense of control; feeling you have little or no control in a situation

STEP THREE: Identify your "tells." We all have habitual responses when we're activated, but they differ from person to person. Ned, for instance, found himself irritated with a student's questions one day—which was notable because it so rarely happens. He recognized it as a tell that he was becoming anxious, and then realized, *Oh yeah, this kid has pretty severe anxiety. It must be rubbing off on me.* Other tells might be high emotion or something more physical, like flushing. This step encourages self-awareness, and practicing it makes you more cognizant of when you're likely spreading stress to others.

STEP FOUR: Claim some space. You probably remember the advice given to new and expectant parents that if a fussy baby can't be soothed, and if the parent is frustrated and stressed, the best thing to do is to put the baby somewhere safe and leave the room until calmer. This advice is meant to reduce the risk that a parent will lose control and shake their baby. While a dramatic example, it's also a clear one: When you're emotionally activated, claim some space so you don't cause damage.

When you recognize that you're anxious, you don't have to hide it. Like we said, you can't. With older kids, you can explain stress contagion to them. "I have a sensitive system," you might say. "When I'm around a lot of stress I tend to absorb it, so I need a few minutes to collect myself, and then I'll be ready to talk about this." Or you might say, "I am really in a terrible mood. I'm not upset with you. But I'm having a really hard time, and I need to be alone to process." Or, "I am really stressed by the news that you shared. That's not your fault. That's on me, and I really appreciate that you shared. Can you give me a few minutes to process this so I can have a conversation that isn't about *my* feelings?" And if you don't catch yourself soon enough and lose your temper, simply apologize: "My self-control is shot. I'm exhausted and fried. Sorry I snapped. I want you to know this is not about you." If you think about it, this is a great way to model what you want your kids to do too. How emotionally healthy would it be for your kid to say, "Mom, I'm not mad at you, but I'm in a bad place right now and need some time to myself."

STEP FIVE: Face, and challenge, your own fears. In the moments you are most anxious, try to identify what fears you have. Is it that your kid won't go to college? Is it that they'll get into a car accident if you let them drive to a football game? Is it that they'll grow up to be a jerk? Facing our fears is some of the hardest work we need to do as parents, and probably one of the most important things we can do to be the best possible parents. So, in this section, we want you to think of what your greatest fears are, and take some time to challenge your thinking around those fears.

What do you most fear would happen if your child doesn't do well?

_____

_____

_____

_____

_____

_____

_____

How likely is that fear to come to pass?

_____

_____

_____

If it did come to pass, what would you do to cope, or to handle it?

_____

_____

_____

_____

_____

_____

_____

_____

Would you be able to make peace with it? How so or how not?

_____

_____

_____

_____

_____

_____

_____

_____

When you think about your values, in what ways do your fears conflict with them? In what ways do they align?

_____

_____

_____

_____

_____

_____

_____

_____

Three helpful reminders when it comes to fear:

1. As we discussed in Principle 2, while, of course, a parent's role is to guide their child, it's ultimately the child's life. Remembering this is an incredibly effective way to lower your anxiety. It's also great for your kid because it conveys respect for them as someone who is in the process of becoming the individual they want to be. You can't possibly control every twist and turn of your child's life; you're not supposed to. It's not your life, and, we suspect, you want them to create a life that they want and will be happy with. You're being asked to do the hardest thing imaginable, which is to separate your own happiness from what's going on with your kids. But if you take their worries on, you're not helping them. Remember that your responsibility as a parent is to love your kids unconditionally and support them as much as you can—not to make sure that they turn out a certain way. (A middle-aged adult we know recently told his parents, "I'm so grateful to you for not having a plan for my life." Aspire to have your kids say that to you one day!) And the more you manage your own anxiety about your kids, the more you can communicate confidence that they can handle their challenges.

2. All our worry about our kids is about the future. We worry that they'll get stuck in a negative place and not get better—or get worse. In our experience, though, if *parents* don't get stuck in a pattern of fear-based responding, *kids* usually don't stay stuck. They go through stuff and then they get out of it. We can't tell you how many kids we've worked with over the years who were a hot mess at age seven, eleven, sixteen, or twenty-one—but turned out great. The slow development of the prefrontal cortex is part of the explanation, as is the fact that there are so many influences on kids' lives that aren't us.

3. We want our kids to develop brains that are capable of coping. As we mentioned in the Introduction, when something stressful happens, we want them to activate the prefrontal cortex, which will keep their stress response in check so they can figure out what to do. Think about it: If you're in a challenging situation but know how to handle it, it's not very stressful because you're able to cope effectively. If something is happening and you don't know how to deal with it, though, that's what's *really* stressful. In these situations, the stress response often becomes so strong that it makes it hard for the prefrontal cortex to do its job and, as a result, you can feel helpless, overwhelmed, and panicked. When kids have repeated experiences of successfully managing tough situations, it conditions their brains to go into "coping mode" when something stressful happens, instead of trying to avoid those situations or freaking out in them. And the more they practice coping, the better they'll be at it, and the more confidence they'll develop in their ability to handle their life. After all, no one learns to handle hard feelings without having hard feelings.

The experience of successfully managing stressful situations leads to a strong sense of control—which "inoculates" you from the harmful effects of stress.

STEP SIX: This step has two components—emergency and preventative—which together help you get rid of at least as much stress as you absorb. There's no better way to become a nonanxious presence than to make sure you're not taking in more stress than you are expelling—because accumulating stress never leads to good things. This is where self-care comes in. And while self-care has gotten a bad rap lately, we think it's misunderstood. Self-care is not necessarily about buying a spa treatment. It's about managing and recovering from acute stress ("emergency medicine") and about developing practices that, over time, prevent the buildup of stress ("preventative medicine").

Regarding emergency medicine, it might indeed be a spa treatment if you can afford it! But it might also be a walk, mindful breathing, a massage, a conversation with a friend, thirty minutes watching your favorite show, journaling, or cooking. And the more demands life throws your way, the more work you will need to do to mitigate the impact of those demands. It seems unfair—how are you supposed to find time to breathe at the hardest times? But this is when it's the most impactful to set whatever boundaries you need to in order to take that time.

You can think of it like being an athlete, who, during an intense season, has to spend *more* time focusing on what happens off the field/ice/pool. You cannot perform your best under pressure unless you've had the fuel, rest, and recovery that you need. No one wins a gold medal by *not* taking rest days.

The preventative medicine part refers to practices that you do regularly, whether you feel like it or not, because you're less stressed and anxious when you do. These include exercising regularly, taking a yoga class once or twice a week, and/or developing a regular meditation practice. These practices can make our amygdala (and the rest of our brain's stress response system) less sensitive and reactive, and can increase the connections between the prefrontal cortex and the amygdala. As we'll discuss more in the next chapter, we believe that meditation is becoming even more important in a world that is increasingly fast-paced and stressful, as it's a powerful tool for helping us become a nonanxious presence. A couple of years ago, a whole police department in a suburb of Washington, D.C., learned Transcendental Meditation (TM), which we both practice. The chief of police practiced TM regularly for three months, but then got busy and stopped. A few weeks later her daughter said to her, "Mom, you need to start meditating again. You're a much better mother when you meditate!" Her daughter recognized the benefit she gains from having a nonanxious presence in the family.

Exercise: Practicing Responses

As we said, becoming a nonanxious presence is a *practice*. You will undoubtedly have many opportunities to work on it, but we've created some scenarios that might come up for you—or that might have already:

1. You're at the airport with your family. It's an absolute madhouse, lines are long, people are grumpy. You're hot and sweaty and tired, and you're doing your best to keep track of everyone's bags, strollers, car seats. Your seven-year-old is rattled about the trip, and when you get to the front of the security line, she doesn't want to put her backpack on the conveyer belt. She's going to hold up the line if you don't get her to comply. How do you respond?

_____

_____

_____

2. You are in the front passenger seat of the car, teaching your fifteen-year-old how to drive. It's to be his first time on a busy street. He's been okay on side streets, but you're plainly terrified to take the next step. What do you do?

_____

_____

_____

3. Your middle schooler is in hysterics because some girls in her class were truly awful to her. You're outraged on her behalf, and her tears are touching off a lot of memories of your own peer drama. How do you respond?

_____

_____

_____

4. Your eleven-year-old is angry at you, claiming you intentionally embarrassed him in front of his friends. What do you do?

_____

_____

_____

5. You're mad at your kid for continuing to make a lot of noise while you're trying to work, and have asked him to keep it down. What do you say?

_____

_____

_____

What are scenarios that are likely to come up in your life?

_____

_____

_____

What are the outcomes you want?

_____

_____

_____

How would a nonanxious presence handle this?

_____

_____

_____

Where might being a nonanxious presence fall apart for you?

_____

_____

_____

Can you think of scenarios in the past year in which responding with a nonanxious presence might have been more helpful than the way it went down?

_____

_____

_____

_____

_____

_____

_____

You will probably lose your temper at some point, or let your anxiety seep through and spread the stress contagion. When this happens, don't let it make you *more* anxious. So much good can come from messing up if you own up to it and apologize. Your kid then gets to see you as a fallible human, which we all are. They get to see how someone takes responsibility for their actions. They get to see what self-compassion looks like, and they'll have the opportunity to practice forgiveness.

Changing the Energy

INSTEAD OF THIS	THINK THIS
This is the worst possible outcome.	This might be what he needs for his growth.
He will never succeed now.	No one really knows how his life will work out.
I need to do more to help!	I'm doing enough. Sometimes I just need to listen.

We don't always know what's in our kids' best interest, in part because what seems to be a terrible mistake often leads to something good in unexpected ways.

What to remember to help you be a nonanxious presence:

Ideally, home is a "safe base."

We can help kids more if we stay calm when they're upset.

Stress is contagious, but so is calm.

All kids go through rocky times as part of their growth and development.

When our kids aren't doing well, most of the work that needs doing is on ourselves.

We want our kids to face life courageously, not fearfully.

We want to radiate calm and courage.

If we don't get stuck in negative patterns trying to change kids, they usually don't stay stuck in a negative place.

For all we know, what's happening with your child is exactly what's supposed to be happening—it's a part of their path/growth. Adopting this mindset allows us to practice what's called "radical acceptance": We accept things as they are this moment—even as we do everything we can to make them better.

 **Cross-Check:**

Principle 1—*Put Connection First*

Principle 2—*Be a Consultant, Not a Boss or Manager*

PRINCIPLE

7

Encourage "Radical Downtime"

In the years leading up to the pandemic, we watched with dismay as the pace of life got faster and faster. We don't need to tell *you*—we know you felt it too. You also probably felt some nostalgia for days of old, when there was often little to do after school or on the weekends unless a friend appeared on your doorstep and asked if you wanted to hang out. Over the years, as life became more scheduled and we all began to fear falling behind, our kids didn't play or casually hang out with friends like we used to—instead, their schedules became filled with tutoring, practices, rehearsals, test prep, jobs, and all-class birthday parties. (And we're the ones arranging these activities, figuring out how they'd get there and back, and working overtime to pay for them.) And then when they had rare cracks of unscheduled time, there was homework to do, texts to respond to, Snapchats to send. *When did kids get so busy?*

The COVID-19 pandemic made a lot of people *more* stressed and tired, not to mention sick and sad. But if there was a silver lining, other than that we got to hear birds again in big cities, it was that life slowed down for most people. Practices, rehearsals, birthday parties—all canceled. Families could have dinner together more nights than before. Adolescents got the sleep they needed for the first time in years. We finally got to watch full seasons of *Law and Order: Special Victims Unit*. As vaccinations became available and restrictions began to lift, many people said, "I'm not going back to that pre-pandemic pace, ever."

We did, though. We didn't alter anything about how we'd been living before, except maybe some adults got more flexibility around remote work. Our kids are busier than ever. We did not learn to slow down, not really, and neither did they.

And oh, how we need to.

In *The Self-Driven Child*, we discussed the toll that the increasingly fast pace of our lives and the decreasing amount of our physical and mental rest have taken on our peace and happiness, on our attention spans and productivity, and on our children's physical health and mental well-being. We pointed out that the balance of rest and activity that is seen in all of nature has been disturbed in human life by advances in technology, beginning with the electric light. Today, the new normal is to be stimulated electronically for much of the day, with few periods of unplugged time, and for both adolescents and adults to sleep between 25 percent and 40 percent less than is necessary to not feel tired during the day. Several recent books have discussed the ways in which our increasing engagement with technology has shortened our attention spans and increased our levels of stress and anxiety. As Gloria Mark's studies have shown, our attention spans when we're online have shrunk from two and a half minutes in 2004 to forty-seven *seconds* over the last few years. This is due to constant task-shifting and multitasking, both of which raise blood pressure and increase other physiological markers of stress, as well as self-perceived stress levels.

Given the unprecedented levels of anxiety and depression in children, teens, and adults, we need to turn this ship around by restoring a healthy balance between rest and activity. This will require that we, and our kids, spend more time during the day (and during the night) in what we call "radical downtime."

Remember that old adage "silence is golden"? It sounded boring when we were teenagers, but today it makes a lot of sense, especially when we consider how crucial sleep is to our physical and mental well-being, how important quiet times are for creativity, problem-solving, and self-reflection, and the extremely wide-ranging benefits of a regular meditation practice. Sleep, meditation, and daydreaming or mind wandering are "radical" forms of downtime because, unlike time-honored downtime activities such as watching TV, listening to music, playing cards or board games, doing woodwork, or gardening, during radical downtime we appear to be doing absolutely nothing—and certainly nothing productive. We think of radical downtime as a brain bath. It cleanses us and leaves us feeling fresh and ready to face whatever's next.

This chapter gives you ideas about how to increase radical downtime in your life and in your child's life. And because half of the battle here is modeling, this chapter focuses a lot on you.

Let Your Mind Wander

In *The Self-Driven Child*, we cited a study that found that 64 percent of young men and 15 percent of young women chose to self-administer a mild electric shock after sitting alone with their thoughts for only six minutes—rather than continuing to sit for an additional nine minutes. Not an entire day, not an hour, but *six minutes*. We don't know how to *be* without stimulation, and yet when we are, we often have great, creative ideas.

We make connections between thoughts. We experience gratitude, and empathy, and we sort through questions about who we are and what matters to us. We *reflect*.

We need this time, and our kids need this time, and it's been overtaken by overly packed schedules and technology that's always there, willing to be our mild electric shock.

A little brain-science context: As neuroscientist Mary Helen Immordino-Yang has said, when we rest, we are not idle. When we sleep, when we let our minds wander, and when we practice certain forms of meditation, we activate the brain's default mode network (DMN). The DMN, which has been called "the genius lounge" and "the imagination network" and uses 80 percent of the brain's energy, is the brain's resting state, as it only activates when we're not focused on a particular task. It includes brain regions that are involved in self-reflection, including circuits that reflect on our past and that enable us to think about the future. In the default mode, our minds wander, and we're able to make connections and generate insights that don't happen when we're task-focused. It thus plays a big role in creativity, problem solving, and the processing of emotions. In young people, the self-reflection produced when the DMN activates is also important for the development of empathy and a coherent sense of identity. This is because when a child or teen hurts a friend's feelings, they need to have time to reflect on the situation in order to learn from it. Also, if kids don't have time to think about their past and imagine their future, it's hard for them to have a deep understanding of who they are. When we—and our kids—are constantly looking for something to focus our attention on, we're missing out on the activation of this really important part of our brain.

We can't always live in the DMN, though, nor would it be good for us if we could. Ideally, we want to be able to toggle efficiently between focusing on tasks and activating the DMN. People who have trouble sustaining attention tend to spend too much time with a wandering mind, "lost" in the DMN, and people who tend to ruminate and obsess about things also spend too much time in the DMN, painfully locked in self-reflection. We want our brains to be capable of both focus and openness, and of going back and forth so that we are not just doers and we are not just daydreamers, but a mix of both. These days, we don't worry about people getting lost in the DMN as much as we worry about them not activating it enough.

Let's do an inventory:

What's the longest period you went today without technology? How about in the last week?

_____

_____

_____

How much time have you had today that's been spent not doing much at all? Not focused on any particular task, just "in your head"?

_____

_____

_____

How much time have you had today that's been spent only on *one* task (for example, cleaning the dishes—not cleaning the dishes while also listening to music and making lunches)?

_____

_____

_____

Reflection questions:

▶ Are you surprised by your answers?

_____

_____

_____

▶ Does it feel like enough?

_____

_____

_____

Below we've included some exercises for enabling the DMN-activated mind wandering that is so important:

Exercise 1: Once a week, go for a walk outside, by yourself. Do not listen to music. Do not talk to anyone on the phone. Do not *bring* your phone at all if you possibly can. Let your mind wander. If it's been a long time since you've gone on a walk without headphones, start with just ten minutes. Or can you go for fifteen? Even thirty? Start small and build up the minutes.

Exercise 2: If you're a parent who feels more like a chauffeur, use some of your driving time to activate your DMN. No radio, no music, no talking. Of course, you still need some of your focus for the road. But try not to do anything *else*. If your kids are in the car with you, suggest that they do the same. No games on their phones. Suggest that perhaps you don't even talk for a little bit, but just embrace the silence.

Exercise 3: Two or three times a week, spend a few minutes thinking about what you're grateful for. Perhaps start by thinking about a relationship in your life that brings you joy, and why that is.

On a scale of 1 to 8, how hard were these exercises for you to do?

1   2   3   4   5   6   7   8

What, if anything, made it hard?

_____

_____

_____

_____

_____

_____

_____

_____

_____

_____

Regardless of how hard or easy it was for you, how did you feel afterward?

_____

_____

_____

_____

_____

_____

_____

_____

There are a lot of activities besides driving with minimal traffic and walking during which you can let your mind wander a bit. Examples will be different for everyone but include:

Jogging

Sitting in a car/Uber/airplane/train/waiting room without reading or talking

Showering

Coloring

Knitting or other needlework where you are not following a pattern

Washing dishes

Yardwork you've done a million times before

Looking at clouds

Looking at stars

The keys to all of these activities are: (1) they're so familiar that you don't really need to concentrate on them and can think about other things, and (2) they don't involve multitasking. We love audiobooks as much as the next person, but gardening without *also* listening to one is restorative. Doing dishes without the TV on is restorative. Driving without the radio or Spotify is restorative. Just try it. Notice how it feels. Note how *you* feel afterward and if it gets any easier the more you do it. This doesn't mean that you should never listen to Spotify or have the TV on while you're working. It just means that you should have enough mental downtime to offset the mind-racing, mind-scattering, and often mind-numbing effects of technology on the brain.

How to Get Your Kids to Let Their Minds Wander

You can't force daydreaming or mind wandering, but you can create situations where it's more likely to happen. Whether we're ten or eighty, it's so tempting to fill silence with words, to fill downtime with tasks, to fill extra space with stimulation. What if you just *don't?* What if you say, "I'm trying to become more comfortable with quiet, and to see how I feel"?

What if you don't fill every hole in your child's schedule?

Most parents will say, "If they are home and not at practice or doing something productive with their time, they'll be on their phone or playing video games, and it's not good for them to be plugged in so much of the time."

We hear this point a lot, and it's a valid one. Parents are so worried about kids spending time counterproductively that they proactively fill it up. But what if you worked out with them short periods when they're not plugged in? What if, together, you build in time for them to be technology-free, and to figure out what they're going to do with an hour—or even twenty minutes? It doesn't necessarily mean they'll daydream—*that* you can't require. They might read or do their hair or a chore that they're so accustomed to that they don't need to think about it much. But at least you're building in the cushion for them to maybe, just maybe, stare out the window for a little while.

It's not easy for a family to be less scheduled. We *want* our kids to be engaged in activities they love. Some kids thrive with a very busy schedule, as long as they have times during the day that are unplugged (like when they're showering, falling asleep at night, or sitting in the car without stimulation). Other kids crave downtime and become very stressed if they can't come home and play or space out for a while before commit- ting to something else. We often oversubscribe kids so they'll do "something productive" and stay off their phones—but crowding up their schedules and creating stress may then add to their being on their phone as a maladaptive stress release.

You may have a good idea as to what your child wants, but if you don't, ask.

Do they think they have enough downtime?

_____

_____

_____

Do they feel too busy? Too pressured?

_____

_____

_____

Like they have no time to themselves?

_____

_____

_____

The key, then, is to help them develop a schedule—ideally within the context of a family goal of everyone having a schedule that works for them. It's also okay for you to say, "You know what? This many activities won't work for the downtime *I* need."

Yet before we can convince kids to be okay with doing less, *we* have to be. We hear a lot of parents say things like, "But I want to make sure he's getting exercise." Great, but does that have to be on three soccer teams? Why not just one—and create a bit more potential downtime? Does your daughter really need voice lessons and piano lessons, or can she choose just one? And, while there are certain social commitments you need or want to commit to, are there some you can say no to and instead use the time for radical downtime? That's how we get to create our spaces of quiet.

It's important to mention that for some people, being in their own head is painful because they're met with unhappy or anxious thoughts. If this sounds familiar, that doesn't mean the answer is to stay busy and keep up the noise at all costs. On the contrary, it's valuable to identify the discomfort so that you can address it—either by doing things on your own to bring down your anxiety, or by seeking help from a therapist.

Getting More Sleep

There's practically a whole cottage industry for helping kids and adults get more sleep. There's a reason for that: Sleep is incredibly important, and getting the right amount and quality of it, and inducing the young people in your life to do so, too, is *hard*. If it's something you and your family struggle with, we feel you. If you're one of the lucky ones, we envy you. If you don't know which camp you fall in, let's explore:

▶ How long does it take you to fall asleep? If you often nod off when it's not bedtime, it's a pretty clear sign you're not getting enough sleep.

▶ How many hours of sleep do you get a night? (See the chart on the next page for ideals—Are you in the ballpark?)

_____

▶ Do you get drowsy during the day? Feel like you need to nap? If yes, it doesn't take a doctor to tell you that you probably need more sleep at night.

_____

▶ How do you feel when you wake up in the morning? You don't have to jump out of bed dancing, but if you feel like you're clawing your way out of an avalanche of snow each morning, common sense says you're probably not getting enough rest.

_____

▶ What's most affected when you don't get enough sleep (e.g., your mental clarity, mood, vulnerability to anxiety, appetite, relationships, productivity)?

_____

▶ How consistent are your bedtime and wake-up time?

_____

▶ If you *wanted* to, could you get to sleep an hour earlier? If so, what changes would you have to make?

_____

Now, let's turn to your child:

▶ How many hours of sleep does your child get?

_____

▶ How rested do you think your child is?

_____

▶ What has and hasn't worked to help get them into bed?

_____

RECOMMENDED HOURS OF SLEEP, BY AGE

Preschoolers	10–13 hours
Ages 6–13	9–11 hours
Ages 14–17	9–10 hours
Ages 18 and up	7–9 hours

While you might be doing fine, and your kids might be too, statistics suggest that most people will find room for improvement. Studies have shown, for instance, that 50 percent of teens fifteen or older sleep less than seven hours a night (whereas they need between nine and ten hours, on average, not to feel tired the next day). And the Centers for Disease Control and Prevention reports that about one in three American adults aren't getting the sleep they need. This is a real problem because:

▶ Sleep deprivation is a form of chronic stress.

▶ You have less emotional control if you're sleep-deprived.

▶ Sleep loss makes your outlook on life more negative.

▶ Sleep deprivation can contribute to anxiety disorders, mood disorders, and substance use disorders.

▶ Sleep deprivation negatively impacts your physical health.

▶ Sleep loss weakens attention, learning, and memory.

▶ Sleep and learning/grades are closely related.

You can't force kids to sleep—we all know that. But just as with mind wandering, you can create sleep-friendly conditions and environments. And it starts with modeling. Kids tell us all the time that their parents don't sleep much either. We've had countless rueful parents shrug in response and say, "What can I do? There just aren't enough hours in the day."

We'll go on record now and say that, in most circumstances, we just don't buy that. You can have an incredibly busy life and still get between seven and eight hours of sleep a night. It's also the most logical choice: You will be more efficient and healthier, and your relationships will improve (see arrows above with regard to sleep and mood disorders/negativity bias/emotional control). When you model good sleep habits, your kids are more apt to adopt them. There are very few excuses for not prioritizing sleep. There are normal obstacles to sleep that have nothing to do with intention, like pregnancy and raising infants, and we take sleep disorders very seriously. If you or your child are trying to get the sleep you need but are unable to because you have insomnia, frequent nighttime awakening, or sleep-related breathing problems, please see a doctor.

Assuming, though, that you're not dealing with any of these circumstances, begin your pursuit of sleep wellness *as* a family. We see so many parents who are always trying to get their kids to go to sleep on time but have their own sleep issues. Make staying well-rested a family goal. Sit with your kids and make a schedule for the week. Don't start the calendar by putting in appointments and assignments. Start the calendar by putting in *sleep times first*, and try to make your sleep and wake-up times as consistent as possible. Then work backward from there to fit everything else in. In this way, you are signaling your family's commitment to sleep.

Your calendar might look something like this:

CALENDAR

Sunday	Sunday night sleep time: 10 p.m.–7 a.m.
Monday	7:45 a.m.: leave for school/work 3:40 p.m.: school's out 4–6 p.m.: soccer practice 6:30 p.m.: dinner 7–9 p.m.: homework and TV 9 p.m.: wind-down time / radical downtime Monday night sleep time: 10 p.m.–7 a.m.
Tuesday	7:45 a.m.: leave for school/work 3:40 p.m.: school's out 4–6 p.m.: homework and TV 6:30 p.m.: dinner 7–9 p.m.: event at school 9 p.m.: wind-down time / radical downtime Tuesday night sleep time: 10 p.m.–7 a.m.

What if a soccer game goes until 9:30? What if there's homework on top of that? What if their best friend is in a play and they want to go to support them, but it means getting a little less sleep? Soccer matters, homework matters, friendship matters, but sleep matters most. Of course, there will be weeks when the schedule is more packed, but if they can't get nine hours every night, can they get eight hours *most* nights? And if not, what else can go? Help your child learn how and when to say no, and that it's okay not to do *everything*. When we shared this with a mom, she laughed and said, "I still haven't learned that lesson." This is the same mom who is also apt to shrug and tell us she's only getting five hours of sleep because there aren't enough hours in the day.

A key learning in adolescence is what to prioritize and what to say no to.

We're not in favor of making sleep a power struggle, in part because you can't make a kid sleep, and in part because fighting about the same thing over and over is terrible for your relationship with your child. And we want to emphasize that learning to regulate the balance between sleep and activity is a long-term goal. (We still haven't completely nailed it!) We believe that the best strategy is to work with your kids to find a bedtime—and sleep habits—that work for them, but to agree on limits within that structure. With younger children, we can tell them that the goal of sleep is for them not to feel tired the next day. We can let them know that some people need more sleep than others, that it's harder for some kids to fall asleep on the early side than it is for others, and that some kids take longer to fall asleep than other kids—even if they go to bed on the late side. Telling kids that we won't know the right bedtime for them until they've tried some different options is one way of getting their buy-in to "experiment" and see what works best for them. For children who are "night owls" and have trouble falling asleep early enough to be adequately rested, a melatonin supplement can be helpful for resetting their biological clock and inducing drowsiness. However, please consult with your pediatrician before trying it.

With most preteens and teens who'd love to stay up as late as possible, we generally recommend that, rather than telling them they need to go to bed and getting into an argument night after night, we say something like, "It's ten p.m. I know you hate being tired in the morning, so I'm going to trust you to go to bed when you need to. Just remember you have to be up at seven a.m., so if you go to sleep now, that would give you nine hours." This approach, which is based on our belief that kids don't like feeling tired—and more generally want their lives to work—is effective with many kids.

▶ How might this work with your kids? Is it likely they would eventually get the idea that it helps them to go to bed on time? Or would the lures of technology make it more likely that you'd find them face down in front of a screen when you get up in the morning?

_____

_____

_____

_____

_____

With kids who don't have the requisite self-regulatory skills to get themselves to go to bed even though they should, we suggest agreeing on a rule regarding what time in the evening they'll be in their room for good—without a phone—and then supporting their reading or listening to a story or a relaxation CD (old school) if it helps them fall asleep.

Ideally, we negotiate boundaries with kids that seem reasonable to them and to us, and we then are consistent about what we're willing to do and not do, as we discussed in Principle 5. Some boundaries that parents, and at least some kids, have found reasonable:

- No use of the car unless you've gotten enough sleep. (This one can be nonnegotiable.)

- No technology an hour before bedtime. (Ideally, kids develop a nightly wind-down routine that includes things like a bath or shower, reading for pleasure, or playing quietly.)

- No phones in the bedroom overnight—and that goes for parents too. (We recommend that kids make an agreement with their friends not to call or text after their bedtime so they don't have to worry about missing out on something important or not being there when a friend needs them.)

Let's Meditate

There's a reason why there's so much talk these days about meditation. Research has shown the many benefits of mindfulness meditation, including improved attention, working memory, cognitive flexibility, and emotional regulation. Moreover, hundreds of studies of Transcendental Meditation have demonstrated its ability to improve attention, learning and other cognitive functions, academic performance, and the physical and mental health of adolescents and adults. A recent study reports that the anxiety levels of medical professionals working in hospitals during the pandemic who learned TM decreased on average by 50 percent in two weeks. Another recent study found that medical students who practiced TM regularly reported gaining an extra two to five hours of productive time each day—despite spending forty minutes meditating—because of the increased mental clarity and mental energy it provides. In our view, meditation may be the ultimate brain bath.

We've written about meditation in our previous books (and mentioned it in our discussion of nonanxious presence in Principle 6 of this one), and we have only a few points to make here. First, mindfulness meditation and Transcendental Meditation are very different practices; the terms "mindfulness" and "meditation" are not interchangeable. Mindfulness meditation usually involves focusing on the breath, intentionally noticing thoughts as they arise, and then letting the thoughts go. In contrast, the TM practice involves the use of a mantra, which one thinks effortlessly, and it does not require being aware of anything (except noticing when you're not thinking the mantra—so you can start it again). Also, while meditation practices that involve maintaining mental awareness are good for the brain in many ways, they don't activate the default mode network, whereas practices like TM *do* activate the DMN because they don't require intentionally maintaining awareness.

Second, most of the kids we see who are taught mindfulness practices in school use them as emergency medicine (for example, to deal with negative feelings), whereas TM is practiced more as preventative medicine. Ideally, TM is done twice a day, whether one feels the need or not, because of the ways that regular meditation improves the functioning of the brain and body.

Third, although there are hundreds of avenues for learning mindfulness meditation (and dozens of mindfulness practices), TM is learned from a certified instructor, and is practiced the same way all over the world.

Fourth, parents of anxious adolescents who know that we both meditate often ask us, "How can I get my kid to meditate?" Our first response is usually to say that we should work with educators to get meditation periods built into the school day, as most teenagers don't want to meditate unless at least some of their friends are. For parents of kids who aren't interested, we recommend that the parents develop a meditation practice for themselves first, in order to model this form of self-care for their children. When parents meditate, their kids are likely to notice changes, which can increase their own openness to learning. We also suggest that, rather than continually telling kids all the great things they're noticing from meditation, parents periodically make offhand comments about these things ("I finished something in the late afternoon in ten minutes that would have taken me a half hour if I hadn't meditated first"), which their kids may or may not pick up on.

We also suggest that parents get their child's buy-in to talk a little bit about meditation, and if the teen is open to it, describe how they think it would help. Parents could then say something like, "We obviously couldn't make you meditate. But we'd love to see you try it for six weeks and see if it can be an 'ally' for you."

Fifth, we can't teach you how to do TM in this book because

you need to learn it from a certified teacher, and we don't practice mindfulness meditation ourselves—and thus can't be of much help in teaching you this practice either. What we can do is ask you to do the following:

Reflect on your own experience with meditation or that of other people you know. Have you seen benefits in yourself or others? If you don't meditate currently, if you felt that you had the time, would you like to? How do you think it might help you?

If you'd like to practice meditation but don't, what keeps you from doing it? Is that obstacle insurmountable? Could you devote twenty minutes twice per day to meditation if you knew you'd gain much more than that in increased productivity?

If you want to explore meditation further, we recommend the following resources:

For mindfulness: apa.org/topics/mindfulness/meditation

For TM: tm.org

 **Cross-Check:**

Principle 1—*Put Connection First*

Principle 5—*Motivate Your Kids Without Trying to Change Them*

Principle 6—*Be a Nonanxious Presence in Your Family*

AN OVERLAPPING PRINCIPLE:
Give Kids More Control in School

I t's one thing to encourage a child's sense of control when they're little and at home with you most of the time, when the cogs and systems of the wider world are somewhat kept at bay. A child can decide what to play with, what sippy cup to drink out of, and which friend to have over for a playdate. As young kids grow older, there's still plenty parents can do to nurture a strong sense of control, but there's a new obstacle: the world of school. More often than not in the school setting, it feels like control is taken out of everyone's hands—yours, your kid's, *and* the teacher's.

Remember that a sense of control has two dimensions: (1) a *subjective* sense of autonomy and confidence in one's ability to handle life's challenges, and (2) the *brain state* that supports this subjective sense, wherein the prefrontal cortex regulates the amygdala. So it follows that schools have two corresponding ways to help students: (1) by supporting their experience of autonomy, and (2) by adjusting school schedules, curricula, and homework and grading policies to minimize the extent to which students are chronically tired and stressed, thereby allowing their brains to function optimally. This is important stuff because research shows that students' sense of autonomy (and their academic motivation) gets lower every year from kindergarten through high school graduation, and because by the time kids get to high school, most are usually tired and stressed.

It's not surprising *why* students' sense of control gets lower every year they're in school. Most of what is communicated to kids is what is expected of them or what they are required to do, with little emphasis placed on student choice or input into decision-making. Also, nap time, play, and recess for younger students have been reduced or eliminated, and adolescents face heavy homework loads, packed school schedules, and extracurricular expectations that are seemingly designed to cause stress and sleep deprivation. Moreover, athletics are reserved for only the most competitive, depriving most kids of the sense of control that physical exercise supports, and the joy-creating, stress-busting pastimes that were once, well, *fun* seem to be monetized and weaponized as "inputs" to résumés and college applications, thereby becoming sources of student stress. With the reduction or complete removal of the things that science shows release stress—sleep, exercise, and play, which kids enjoyed in abundance as young children—the inflows of stress far exceed the outflows. This combination of factors greatly compromises a sense of control by reducing the prefrontal cortex's ability to regulate the amygdala and the rest of the brain's stress circuitry.

The fact is that schools aren't really designed with the brain in mind. We focus on what we want students to learn and how we should teach and evaluate them but give almost no attention to the organ in their body that does the learning. Many of the students we work with cope with their low sense of control by resisting adults' attempts to get them to do what they're "supposed" to be doing, while others resign themselves to having no input into what, how, or why they learn. Just consider that decades of neuroscience research have shown that the optimal brain state for learning is one of *relaxed alertness*, and that the optimal learning environment is one in which there is high challenge but low threat. This is a bit of a problem, as the majority of high school students report being stressed and tired (rather than relaxed and alert) and find school to be boring and stressful (rather than challenging but not threatening) most of the time they're in the classroom. We hate to say it, but rather than making healthy brain development the highest goal of education, the way that many schools currently function is actually harmful to brain development.

For many of our clients, school is a source of considerable stress and suffering because of what neuroscientist Robert Sapolsky calls the "killer combination" of responsibility without control—or high work demands with little autonomy. Just as damaging: These students are missing the chance to develop the healthy sense of control they'll need to thrive not just as teens, but later as adults.

If it seems like we're being overly hard on schools, consider these four data points:

1. A nationwide survey of more than twenty thousand high school students conducted in 2020 (before the pandemic) found that almost 75 percent of the feelings that students reported about school were negative, with the majority of students reporting that they felt tired, stressed, and bored most of the time they were in school.

2. Although there are many sources of student stress, a recent study of students from three high schools in a suburban Midwest district found that the top twelve stressors reported by students were all related to school, grades, academic achievement, and college-related pressures.

3. Student suicides are much lower in the summer and on school breaks than during the school year, particularly on school days.

4. There's currently a very high incidence (up to 15 percent) of school refusal, even in elementary grade students.

Also, consider that medical students, who are among the best-educated people in our society, report shockingly high levels of anxiety and depression (30 percent of medical students and residents suffer from depression). Although the lives of medical students and doctors can be very stressful, we worry that their heightened vulnerability to anxiety and mood-related difficulties is related to the effects that high stress and massive sleep deprivation had on their developing brains while they were high school and college students trying to create a résumé that would get them into medical school. Success and achievement do not protect brains from high stress. Healthy brains protect themselves.

So, what are schools doing about the crisis in student mental health? Rianna Alexander, a high school student in Arizona, who has become an advocate for student wellness, confronted her local board of education about the alarmingly high rate of suicide in their district and the need for more attention to student mental health. In response, she was told that students' mental health problems are rooted in family issues and that "it's not about school." This response infuriated the girl, as she asked herself and others, "How can they say that? I go to school for six hours, have after-school activities, and come home to do homework before and after dinner. School is the last thing I think about as I try to fall asleep and the first thing I think about in the morning. It's all I think about; school is my life!"

Other school systems *are* trying to address students' mental health, often by calling for more services for students, which we applaud. However, this approach misses the point that school itself is, for many students, the major source of stress and suffering in their lives. Instead of focusing solely on treating the problems that school helps to create, we should be changing the ways that education contributes to mental health problems in the first place. As we'll show you later in the chapter, change is achievable, and we can all play a part in it. But first, let's talk about why school has become so stressful for kids, teachers, and parents.

The Cycle of Stress: We're All in This Together

During the question-and-answer period of a talk we gave in 2022 to a thousand students at a high-achieving public high school in Illinois, a student stood up and asked, "Because homework causes so much stress, anxiety, and loss of sleep for kids, should teachers be held responsible for the mental health problems that their homework causes?" Before we could answer her question, every single student in the auditorium stood up, clapped, and cheered. The rafters shook, and the stage we stood on rumbled like we were in the middle of a mild earthquake. "No, definitely not," we said when the kids calmed down. We explained that teachers don't intentionally try to make students' lives miserable by overloading them with homework. Teachers, like students, parents, and administrators, are all part of a flawed system that's currently not working well for anyone.

We talked recently with a stressed-out group of teachers about *why* they engaged in practices that seemed, to us, to be pretty controlling, like pressuring parents to check in often on their kids' homework and assigning homework that gave students very little choice about how to approach it or when it might be completed. As we got deeper into the weeds about the whats, whys, and wherefores of their approach, one explained, "As you know, the kids have to take these standardized tests. There's tremendous pressure for them to do well because their performance affects the way we're evaluated as teachers, and also the way the administration and the district as a whole are evaluated." Can you imagine a worse scenario from a sense-of-control perspective? This teacher is not taking the test herself, has no control over whether the students slept well the night before, had a healthy breakfast (or any breakfast), what conflicts they may have gotten into in the hours before the test, or whether they were able to focus. This teacher does not have control over what is on the test, its format, or its timing. And yet, the stakes feel very high—and, indeed, *are*. It's no wonder that we have a worrisome rate of teacher burnout, with teachers leaving the profession, on average, after just five years.

In other words, it's not just students who are unhappy. Teachers are often just as stressed and miserable, in part because of the increasingly limited autonomy with which they are allowed to do their jobs. At one conference, twelve hundred educators jumped to their feet in applause when Edward Deci, the codeveloper of self-determination theory, shared research showing the enormous benefits of promoting autonomy in teachers. Teachers, too, want more choice about how they help students meet educational goals. And yet teachers' autonomy has been progressively lessened as the standards-based reform movement has increasingly tried to control what and how teachers teach. School administrators don't have it any easier. They have to respond to pressures from anxious and highly competitive parents, *and* to the dictates from their school district and their state, which are often laid down by legislators who have little knowledge about education—and even less about the brain.

Exercise: How Do We Use Homework?

If you are a teacher, consider this experiment: For one week, for every homework assignment you give, ask yourself:

1. What's the purpose of the assignment? Is it to reinforce the day's lesson? To deepen understanding in kids? To offer extra/optional practice? To meet expectations placed on you by your supervisor, school, or district? To meet expectations or pressure from parents?

_____

_____

_____

2. Do your students have the same understanding of the purpose of the assignment?

_____

_____

_____

3. Once the assignment has been returned, is it something you'd want to assign again and in the same form? Was it worth it?

_____

_____

_____

We are not opposed to homework, and would wager you aren't either. But because you cannot *make* students do homework, it helps when you and your students are on the same page about its purpose.

The bottom line is that we all play a role in this cycle of stress. Consider the case of Karl, a sixth-grade student who isn't doing well in school. His teacher is worried, first because she really likes Karl and wants good things for him. And second, because it reflects badly on her when a student in her class does as poorly as Karl is doing. His scores in math go into her averages and bring her ratings down. She worries that her administrators are judging her for Karl's poor performance.

The teacher writes to Karl's parents and puts pressure on them to get Karl to study. The teacher's worries add to the parents' concerns about Karl's future, and that if he doesn't do well in sixth grade, when the material is relatively easy, he'll struggle mightily when he goes to high school, which will then hurt his college prospects. They worry that the teacher is judging their parenting skills and their oversight of their kid. So they put pressure on Karl, insisting that he sit and do his math homework every evening at five p.m. and denying him his skateboard until he improves his grades.

Karl, meanwhile, is not a fan of math homework because he would much rather be skateboarding. The more his parents pressure him to sit down and focus, the less he wants to. Why doesn't *he* get any say? He hates math, he hates school, he's not crazy about his teacher either as the source of the skateboard-depriving homework, and he sometimes feels like he hates his parents because they won't get off his back. He doesn't have an outlet for his stress or lack of control, so he shuts down in class, which is a way of *asserting* control—by insisting that no one can *make* him do his work. This makes his teacher even more upset. *Time to email Karl's parents again.* And so the cycle continues, looking something like this:

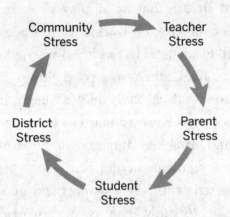

Community Stress

Teacher Stress

Parent Stress

District Stress

Student Stress

Sometimes the circle has different components. At one school where we were talking about the futility of homework at a young age, a teacher said, "The parents all want the kids to have homework. I'm worried I'll get in trouble if I don't assign it." We asked what grade she taught, and, we kid you not, she said, "Kindergarten." And why do the parents feel this way? Because they're afraid, pressured by the thought of fellow parents, whose kids *do* have homework, whose kids *are* being pushed harder, and are therefore leveling up ahead of their kids. *If so-and-so's kid has three hours of homework and mine only has an hour, then the other kid is going to get ahead—and stay ahead—of mine!* A frenzy ensues, and education becomes all about pushing and being more competitive, earlier and earlier. This cycle is crazy-making, and doesn't get anyone anywhere. Relationships fray. *Maybe,* through sheer force of pressure, a slightly better grade results, but at what cost?

And Now for Some Good News

We know that we can do things differently. We've observed many teachers in traditional classroom settings who are taking steps to support their students' autonomy, and who have found that simply asking for their opinions and feedback significantly increases their academic motivation and engagement. And we've worked with educators who are going even farther. For example, we recently visited a public middle school whose principal, Jerry Putt, decided to take matters into his own hands. At his school, which promotes student-directed learning, students can participate in a program in which they spend their afternoons working on projects of their own choosing, which the kids love. The teachers love the program too, in part because they get to function as guides and mentors to their students rather than just imparters of information and discipline keepers. They don't have to continually try to get kids to focus on things that they're not that interested in. When we asked Jerry what motivated him to create this program, he told us, "I'm sixty years old, and I'm simply not going to do anything anymore that's harmful to kids. And a lot of what we do with kids in school is harmful to them. We should be designing schools *for* kids—rather than making them 'do school.' I want people to hold me accountable for what matters, like healthy development and kids' power to change their own trajectory."

Somewhat surprised, we asked Jerry, "You banned homework?"

"Nope," he replied. "I simply said it couldn't be used for grading kids. When I was asked, 'Well, then what's the point of homework?' I responded that that was a good point. So, yeah, now there's basically no homework in the school."

Another school pushing boundaries is Village High School in Colorado Springs, where students play a role in all decision-making regarding academics and the school community. Students work with their teachers and administrators to determine the best ways for them to meet the district's graduation requirements while spending as much time as possible pursuing their own interests. They decide how much learning to do online and how much in the classroom, and they determine the best pace at which to meet their educational goals. When we asked Village students about their experience there, they all said that they were much less stressed, better rested, more motivated, and learning more than they had in a traditional high school or middle school. Similarly, the teachers all said that this was the best teaching job they ever had. By playing the role of guide and mentor, they were able to make a significant difference in students' lives—which was why they went into education in the first place. Presumably for this reason, Village High, unlike many schools, has a waiting list for teachers. When we asked the founder and principal of Village, Nathan Gorsch, how his students perform on standardized state tests, he said that they have the highest scores in their district. When we asked him why he doesn't emphasize this more in the school's marketing materials, he answered, "It's just not what we're about."

These school models might seem radical, but on the contrary, the principles beneath them are widely accepted. The Centers for Disease Control and Prevention (CDC) pushes for student autonomy and empowerment too, suggesting that this powerful government agency sees supporting student autonomy as a public health issue. The CDC holds: "When students feel their teachers are open to their ideas and allow them to make choices regarding their learning and schoolwork, they are more engaged in school, less disruptive in class, and report feeling a stronger sense of belonging and connectedness to their school."

Even at the medical school level, changes can be made to increase student autonomy and reduce their stress. When Stuart Slavin, a pediatrician and expert in medical education, was at Saint Louis University, he tracked the mental health of the medical students there. When he found that the percentage of students who reported the symptoms of generalized anxiety disorder and/or major depressive disorder was perilously high, the university agreed to do a study that felt risky to everyone involved. They reduced the amount of time students spent in class, and therefore the amount of material taught, by 10 percent. Students learned cognitive restructuring strategies for "talking back" to perfectionism and other forms of distorted thinking that are common among highly stressed medical students. In addition, the students were given a half day each week to work on self-selected projects related to their fields of interest as a way of promoting their autonomy and engagement.

At the end of the study, the incidence of anxiety disorders and depression decreased by 80 percent, and the students earned *higher* scores on their medical exams than students had in previous years. It turned out that when students weren't chronically stressed, overloaded, and exhausted, they learned and retained more. Oh, and by the way, they were happier.

For the remainder of this chapter, we'll present ideas for improving the lives of students and educators by showing the places where a sense of control *can* be found, even within a system that isn't designed for it. We explore steps that will improve the lives of kids and educators, what keeps us from taking these steps, and how to get past the barriers. We want parents and educators to be confident that giving kids more control makes sense, that it works, and that it's safe to do it. And at the same time, we recognize that a lot of you might be stuck between a rock and a hard place. You might not love the way you're required to teach, or the school you're able to send your child to, but how are you supposed to buck an entire system?

Herewith we offer some small and some not-so-small changes teachers might make in the classroom to foster a stronger relationship between a student's prefrontal cortex and amygdala, and thus a healthier sense of control. We'll also offer tips for administrators and parents to support a strong sense of control in the young people in their lives.

Everyone: Support Autonomy in the Classroom

Betty, a high school sophomore, and a classmate approached their English teacher one day with a question. They were working on an essay about the novel *Like Water for Chocolate*, and part of the instructions read that you could not use the words "I," "could," "me," "we," or "could have."

"If we make a convincing argument to you as to why we need to use one of those words, can we use it?" Betty asked.

"No," replied the teacher. "The assignment is the assignment."

Now, it seems to us that there were very good reasons for asking students not to use those specific words. The assignment was likely designed to encourage students to be more analytical and less personal in their writing. Or perhaps it was intended to make students think more flexibly about language, like in a game of Taboo. But this teacher didn't explain the rationale. And this teacher didn't hear Betty out.

We get it; teachers have a lot to do. Most teachers reading this would probably say, "If I had to listen to every student argue for why they should be able to do something, we'd never get anything done." Parents have certainly felt this way a million times too. Sometimes it just doesn't feel like there's time for the "whys" and the debates.

But looked at from another perspective, this was a small moment that could have nurtured a sense of control instead of shutting Betty and her classmate down, as the teacher essentially did. Imagine how many small moments there are in a student's day that go this way, and how different they could feel if the adults in their lives handled these moments differently. We believe teachers should, where possible:

1.   Let kids weigh in about classroom rules and expectations. Kids abide by rules that make sense to them.

2.   Remember that the goal is buy-in, not simply compliance, and the brain state of willing engagement. Explain the rationale for specific assignments—or what you hope students will get out of them (exposure to a new idea, reinforcement of

learning, practicing different ways of applying what they've learned).

3. Seek students' feedback about instruction and assignments (Was this helpful to you? Do you think you could have learned it a better way? How long did it take you to do it?), and then incorporate their feedback in designing future instruction and assignments.

4. Give kids choices about how to accomplish learning (such as an individual research project versus a group project).

5. Offer more than one way to demonstrate learning and mastery (an essay, a PowerPoint or multimedia presentation, a poem or song, an illustration or three-dimensional depiction).

6. Instead of mandating the use of certain tools, like note cards, encourage students to find learning strategies that work for them (note cards or another way of taking notes for a paper; reading a math text or learning through an online program like Khan Academy).

7. Teach students that they're responsible for their own learning, which means that if they aren't learning it the way you're teaching it, they should try to find another way.

8. Give kids some choice about what they learn about (for example, what aspects of the Civil War they are most interested in studying) and let them focus strongly on their areas of interest.

9. Make at least some, if not most, homework optional and ungraded. (Our motto is "Inspire but don't require," meaning inspire students to learn at home but don't make most assignments mandatory, which confuses the means for the ends.)

10. Give students time periods during the week to work on self-selected projects even if they're unrelated to the curriculum.

Look at the list above, and whether you are a teacher, parent, or administrator, put a checkmark by the items that you feel uncomfortable with.

For each checkmark, ask yourself three questions:

What about it makes you uncomfortable?

_____

_____

_____

Would you like to change that feeling?

_____

_____

_____

What would need to happen to make it feel safe to try it?

_____

_____

_____

Teachers and Administrators: Make Schools Brain-Healthy Learning Environments

1. Reduce the content taught and the homework load by at least 10 percent (as Slavin's study did). Emphasize the most important concepts and information you want your students to remember. Racing to "cover the curriculum" only increases the amount of information students forget.

2. Support later start times for middle and high school students, or make first period optional, a free period, or a rest period during which they can sleep at their desk or meditate. (We'd rather teach kids for four hours who'd slept for eight than teach kids for eight hours who'd slept for four.)

3. Encourage students to form problem-solving teams to work out solutions to classroom or interpersonal problems.

4. Create teams composed of students, parents, teachers, and administrators focused on helping everyone at the school be better rested and less stressed.

Everyone: Ask for the Evidence

Schools often advertise their use of "evidenced-based practices." Whether you are a teacher, a parent, or an administrator, use that! Let's insist on practices that are supported by evidence. Here is a column of common practices for which there is no evidence, and a column of statements we *do* have plenty of scientific support for:

NO EVIDENCE	STRONG EVIDENCE
Early reading and writing instruction	Research in multiple languages has shown that the most efficient age to teach kids to read is seven, and that any advantage to learning to read early washes out later in childhood. Most children don't have mature enough connections between their brain and the small muscles in their fingers to hold a pencil properly until age six or later.
Early school start times	High school kids need nine to ten hours of sleep not to feel tired. Kids in high-achieving high schools average six hours of sleep.
The use of rewards as primary motivators	Rewards undermine autonomy if used to coerce students to do what we want them to do. A strong sense of autonomy leads to intrinsic motivation and better grades and test scores.
Excessive (more than two hours) of homework for high school students	More than two hours of homework backfires when it comes to learning and contributes significantly to our mental health crisis.
Teaching more than kids can retain	Testing is great, but only if students are able to review their mistakes and learn from them. Otherwise tests are meaningless. Teaching kids more and more content just increases the amount of material they forget within a couple of weeks.

Let's look more closely for a moment at calculus. It used to be that very few kids took calculus in high school; some schools may have offered it for those rare exceptional kids who were born thinking in numbers. Now, any student who sees themselves as high-achieving is encouraged to take calculus in high school—and believes they have to in order to have a successful future. An economics professor who went to Stanford disavows that approach: "A year of precalculus in high school (which lots of kids in my school skipped) gave me a slower, stronger foundation to better understand calculus when I took it for the first time in college. It made sense to me in a way that kids who jumped straight to Calculus AB and BC in high school never got. They struggled when they took calculus again at Stanford. I'm convinced that that slow, deep prep based on key concepts helped more than I realized at the time." And yet, parents still encourage calculus in high school, kids still take it, teachers still teach it, and the circle of stress continues.

It's also true, as we referenced in *The Self-Driven Child*, that what we know about brain development needs to play a role in when we teach kids what. Virtually everything (except a foreign language accent) is easier to learn with a more mature brain. With what we know about the slow development of the prefrontal cortex, it's unlikely that a high percentage of high school students are physiologically *ready* to take calculus.

Parents: Resist Pressure from School to Do What You Know Isn't Right for Your Child

For those parents whose kid's teacher says they need to make their kid do their homework, politely decline. Forward emails about missing work to the student directly. Thank the teacher but let them know that while you are there to support your child, you have learned that the more effort you expend, the less your child does, and that if you take responsibility for something that is your child's, you weaken them. Or if your child is having trouble learning to read and the teacher asks you to make sure your kid reads to you for twenty minutes at night, remember that working on something difficult when you're ready to wind down is never productive. Let the teacher know that it will be more beneficial if your kid works on the hard parts of reading during the day, when fresh—and that you'll read *to* your kid at night. One of the most powerful things you can say as a parent is "This isn't working for my child."

Teachers and Parents: Reduce the Data Dump . . . or at Least Stop Paying So Much Attention to It

Most of you are all too familiar with schools' online portals, where you can see homework assignments and grades in real time, at all times. This is an invitation for many parents to check obsessively, and thus become much more aware and involved in whether their child is completing their assignments and how they're doing on every single test. No, no, and just no. Remind yourself whose problem and responsibility this is, and step away from constant monitoring, no matter what new fancy tool or portal comes along.

We know that different districts and schools have different requirements for these portals, and you may not be able to change the fact that you're expected to post on them (if you're a teacher) and to pay attention to them (if you're a student). But for goodness' sake, stay off them if you're a parent unless your kid specifically *asks* you to look and wants you to provide some backup. Making it their choice about when you look, how often, and what your role is, is a really powerful way to support their sense of autonomy.

Teachers: Be Assertive About What You Know Is Right for Kids

We recognize that it's not simple to break out of the cycle of stress. Teachers don't want to face the wrath of parents who want their young kids to have homework. We get that. But what we recommend to teachers is, be as courageous as you can—because you know things that most parents don't know. When parents of young children are panicking because they're afraid other kids will get ahead of theirs, even if they know that almost one hundred years of research has failed to show that homework contributes to learning in the elementary grades, stand your ground and remember Jerry Putt's line: "I'm not going to do anything anymore that's harmful to kids."

Parents: Help Your Kids Become Good Self-Advocates

We're sure that all the educators reading this book are superb. But there are teachers working with kids who are burned out or otherwise not as helpful as they could be, and there are certainly teachers who are not a good match for certain students. When your kid has a burned-out teacher or one who's not a good match, it can really suck. However, it also offers kids opportunities to develop the muscle of working around a difficult relationship. At the end of the day, what you want your child to learn is how to get to the outcome they want, *in spite of* a bad system, a burned-out teacher, or an ineffective leader.

One of our favorite tools to use in helping kids develop

strong self-advocacy skills was developed by NYU's Gabriele Oettingen, and follows the acronym WOOP, wherein you ask:

What is my **W**ish? It should be something that is achievable, that's within my control.

What is the **O**utcome I want? (How would I feel if I fulfilled my wish?)

What are the **O**bstacles *in me* that keep me from my wish?

What is my if/then **P**lan? *If* the obstacle comes up, *then* what will I do to get closer to fulfilling my wish? What can I tell myself? What can I do?

A colleague, Jay, played this out recently with his son Akhil, who found the way his biology teacher taught to be boring and confusing. When Jay asked Akhil what his wish was, Akhil said, "To get a new biology teacher!" But alas, that wasn't within Akhil's control. This was the school's only biology teacher. Akhil could certainly choose to drop biology, but that would come with consequences to his transcript. Once they talked this through, Jay asked again what Akhil's wish was that he *could* control.

Akhil: "My wish is to finish biology with an A or a B."

Jay: "How would you feel if that happened? What outcome are you looking for?"

Akhil: "I'd be relieved because I'd never have to take bio again!"

Jay: "What are the obstacles that keep you from your wish?"

Akhil: "The obstacle is that Mr. Roberts doesn't make sense most of the time."

Jay: "Let me clarify: What are the obstacles *in you* that keep you from your wish?"

Akhil: "Nothing! I'm showing up and trying, Dad. I'm telling you, Mr. Roberts is the problem here."

Jay: "I'm not doubting that. But there's a tension: You're in a class with a teacher you don't understand, but you can't get out of it and you want a good grade. So it makes sense to focus on what *you* can do."

Akhil: [sigh]

Jay: "So, if for some reason you did fall short of the A or B you want, what do you imagine might be the reason? What might be the thing you did or didn't do that tripped you up? What are the obstacles in you that might keep you from that feeling of having passed biology?"

Akhil: "I guess I've been so mad at Mr. Roberts I haven't looked for other ways to learn the stuff."

Jay: "Okay, if that comes up for you, if you start to feel that way, what could you do? Is there anything you could tell yourself or *do* that would help you get around the obstacle?"

Akhil: "I could think about Mr. Roberts's face when I ace the next test, despite the fact that he thinks I suck at biology. I could think about proving he's wrong about me. And Greg offered to help me understand the stuff that Mr. Roberts teaches so badly, so I guess I could get Greg's help."

Now, try this with your kid the next time they are struggling with a teacher they don't quite gel with:

Can you identify a wish? (Remember, something within your control! We don't have magic wands on hand.)

W:

_____

_____

_____

What's the outcome you want, meaning, what do you want to feel if this wish comes to be?

O:

_____

_____

_____

What are the obstacles within you that would get in the way?

O:

_____

_____

_____

When you encounter an obstacle, what is your plan for moving past it?

P:

_____

_____

_____

Bad school situations like this can be very helpful in enabling your children to learn to advocate for themselves—never an easy thing to do, but an important life skill. When a high school choir club's beloved director moved to another town, the students didn't really care for his replacement. Her style was fairly controlling, whereas their previous director gave them a lot of power in running the program. They didn't have a sense of psychological safety with the new director, who they felt criticized them at every opportunity. They missed their old director's sense of playfulness, as the new director was serious and a bit aloof. And there was a values gap, as the choir club officers believed their main goal was to create an inclusive community, whereas the new choir teacher's main goal was to put on a professional-level performance.

In this situation it looked like there wasn't much that could be done. The parent volunteers for the choir club didn't have any say about who the director was, and it wasn't their place to offer her critical feedback. Plus, it wouldn't have been appropriate for them to swoop in. The whole point was that they wanted the students to feel empowered.

The parents held a meeting with the students in which they gave them space to air their grievances. Just being able to tell trusted adults about all they were carrying, and how they were feeling, was hugely cathartic for the students and enabled them to access the problem-solving part of their brains. The students planned a meeting with the new director for them to air their grievances directly, and the parent volunteers were able to nudge them on a path that they hoped would be more productive. They encouraged the students to send her a letter first so she would not be blindsided. The parents also suggested ways to frame their feedback, and offered some context about what could likely be changed (her willingness to hand some control back to the students) and what couldn't (her lack of playfulness might have just been her personality, and that was okay!).

Unlike in their academic classes, the students had a choice about whether to participate in the choir club, and there was always the possibility that some would not want to anymore. But at least they had the skills to communicate their needs and desires to their new director, and to try to make it work before making a decision either way. And in the end, after several months passed and the director and students got to know one another more, they reached a nice equilibrium, and no kids ended up quitting.

We want to teach our kids to respect authority, but we also want to teach them the best ways to challenge it respectfully if appropriate. For instance, when fifteen-year-old Elizabeth's teacher lost one of her tests, the teacher gave her a choice of either retaking the test or having the test be a blank so that her grade would neither go up nor down.

"Neither of those will work for me," Elizabeth told her teacher, which, when recounted to Elizabeth's mother, made her jaw drop. But while it might seem brazen, Elizabeth explained respectfully to the teacher that she had studied hard for the test, and felt she had done incredibly well. If she had to retake the test, she would likely not do as well because so much time had passed since she'd studied for it. And it didn't seem like a blank score would be fair either because she *knew* that she had done well and her score would have improved her overall grade. And after all, Elizabeth pointed out, it wasn't her fault that the teacher lost the test, so she shouldn't be penalized.

The teacher, to his credit, agreed. He and Elizabeth figured out a way for him to give extra weight to other assignments that showed her mastery of the unit's material. Her grade would reflect the work she'd put in to the class, and the teacher would feel comfortable that he was giving her a grade that she had earned.

Exercise: Think About a Time When You Advocated for Yourself

What did you do well in this exchange? What are you proud of?

_____

_____

_____

What do you wish you had done differently?

_____

_____

_____

If you could give advice to your earlier self about how to approach the situation, what would you say?

_____

_____

_____

Now, share this story with your kid.

Think of a time when you should have advocated for yourself but didn't.

What held you back?

_____

_____

_____

What do you wish you had said or done?

_____

_____

_____

Do you think it would have changed the outcome?

_____

_____

_____

Share this story with your kid too.

Parents and Teachers: Remember That Discipline Means Helping Kids Learn from Their Behavior

When Ned was in seventh grade, his class went on a field trip to a museum. A bunch of his friends went to the gift shop afterward, slipped items into their backpacks, and left without paying for them. In other words, they shoplifted. Ned was never a rule breaker, but on this day he felt bold. He put some erasers and pencils in his backpack and left the shop feeling slightly guilty and slightly elated.

Later, of course, the jig was up when the store contacted the school about all their missing merchandise. Though Ned had not been the most prolific thief by a long shot, he was one of the first to confess. He felt terrible, which was plain for all to see. His mother did not lecture him or ground him. Instead, she calmly explained that he would need to write a letter to the gift shop apologizing for his conduct, and that he would need to use his allowance to replace the stolen items. The school's reaction was similar: They cared very much that Ned apologize and make amends, but they did not consider him a discipline problem or feel they needed to create a "behavioral plan." (We are generally not big fans of behavioral plans in school; we see so many kids who have the same plan year after year, even though nothing changes or gets better.)

Forty years later, Ned still remembers that experience and has never stolen again. If the authority figures in his life had unreasonably punished him, or berated him such that he believed he was a "bad kid," he might well have said, "To hell with you all!" and *become* that bad kid. The best form of discipline allows for natural consequences (you made this error, so now you have to make it right) while keeping a sense of relatedness and respect (you made a mistake but you are not a bad person).

The natural consequences for Ned's error weren't so unmanageable. But as a kid gets older, mistakes can become more costly. For instance, we know of a twelve-year-old who lost his good winter jacket. He had to use his own money to replace it and couldn't go with his friends to play in the snow until he did. We know of a sixteen-year-old who backed his car into a parked car. He had to use his entire earnings from his summer job to repair the damage. Yikes! In some of these expensive situations, parents might want to cushion the consequence, and we're not opposed to that. After all, a $1,000 repair to a kid is a *much* bigger percentage of his income than it is of ours. But we want to avoid protecting kids from natural consequences altogether. This is how learning happens!

The Central Teaching (Pun Intended)

Our final two cents on schools: While parents, politicians, educators, and educational reformers do battle over how much should be asked of kids and what should be taught, more of our attention should shift to *how* to teach our children; we all need to work together to find our way. Remember that teachers (especially veteran ones) have seen *hundreds* of fourth graders or seventh graders, whereas parents may be on their first. With their long view, teachers are not only invested in helping kids learn but also interested in their development as people. Schools are places of learning, but not just academically. For most kids, school is also where they experience growth and growing pains; navigate friendships, conflicts, and emerging and shifting identities; find their potential and limits; and much, much more. In all those domains, learning involves meaningful struggle. And those struggles not only impact but occasionally take a back seat to schoolwork itself. Good teachers understand this truth and help students and parents understand it as well. With a steady hand on the tiller and a steely eye on the horizon, veteran teachers help tots, teens, and parents alike ride out the waves and navigate toward shores that often are not even in view.

Teachers can encourage parents not to be so afraid that a child will fall off a cliff if they don't have piles of homework, or don't do it, or if their grades, friendships, and lives are less than perfect. Parents can support and trust teachers, knowing that the more autonomous teachers are, the happier they will be, and the more invested in and effective with children they'll be. Administrators can make sure to learn basic brain science and share it with their staff, and can fight for policies and a culture that supports a sense of control.

Students can learn to think about their school years not just as a time of building a future of college and work, but of building themselves. A sense of control is as much about developing healthy brains as brilliant futures. With a bigger-picture perspective, kids can more readily accept that they won't like every teacher they have, they won't always be perfect, they won't always find the going easy, and they won't always know what their futures will hold or how they will get there. And, that that's okay. That's how life works.

While most of the hard work is theirs, much of the time children will have adults around them, sometimes seen and sometimes silent, pulling for them. As a client once said to a much younger Ned, you will not understand until you have children of your own how valuable it is to have other adults around your children who want the best for them. How true. As educators with lifetimes of working with kids, we—and your children's teachers—want the best for yours.

Acknowledgments

We'd like to thank the scores of parents who have told us over the years that they want their kids to be self-driven—but found the principles and strategies hard to apply. Many asked us for a book to help them to be sure that giving kids more control is right and is safe to do—and to help them work through the blocks and objections that keep them going back to more "command and control" approaches. This book is our response to their requests.

We owe an enormous debt of gratitude to our dear friend Jenna Land Free, the writer, editor, and mother extraordinaire whose literary skill, insight, and critical eye have helped to make our three books accessible and enjoyable to read. We owe Jenna particular thanks for this book, as her experience as a mother and her discussions with other parents were crucial for creating the exercises in which we invite parents to engage.

We are eternally grateful to the scientists who helped us understand the enormous power of a sense of control, including

Bruce McEwen, Robert Sapolksy, Sonia Lupien, Steve Maier, Richard Ryan, and Edward Deci.

Many, many thanks to our gifted editor at Viking, Laura Tisdel. Her insight, humor, judgment, encouragement, and literary brilliance have made working with her one of the truly rewarding pleasures of our lifetimes. We also want to thank Laura's son, Mark Burton, who patiently worked through the exercises with his mother as we were developing them.

Thank you to the entire team at Viking—from Laura's assistant to the interior and cover design team, to the publicity and marketing groups. Your guidance and gusto are invaluable.

As always, our profound gratitude goes to our incredible agent, Howard Yoon, who saw the potential in our first book and has been a continual source of inspiration, wisdom, advice, and support over the last seven years.

We have many people to thank for contributing their wisdom and experience to the education chapter in this book. These include our friend and colleague Mike Nicholson, and other huge fans of promoting a sense of control in students, including Steve Shapiro, Jerry Putt, Nathan Gorsch, and Katey McPherson.

Finally, a special thanks goes to Riana Alexander, a student and mental health advocate in Arizona. Our interview with Riana inspired us and strengthened our resolve to include a chapter on education in this book.

Notes

INTRODUCTION: How to Use the Seven Principles

xix **It helps them gain control:** M. W. Gallagher, K. Naragon-Gainey, and T. A. Brown, "Perceived Control Is a Transdiagnostic Predictor of Cognitive–Behavior Therapy Outcome for Anxiety Disorders," *Cognitive Therapy and Research* 38 (2014): 10–22, doi.org/10.1007/s10608-013-9587-3.

Lauren Wadsworth et al., "Levels of Perceived Control and Treatment Response in a Brief Partial Hospital Setting," *Neurology, Psychiatry and Brain Research* 34 (December 2019): 1–8, doi.org/10.1016/j.npbr.2019.08.001.

xix **Recent studies have also shown:** L. M. Precht et al., "It's All About Control: Sense of Control Mediates the Relationship Between Physical Activity and Mental Health During the COVID-19 Pandemic in Germany," *Current Psychology* 42 (2023): 8531–9, doi.org/10.1007/s12144-021-02303-4.

Leslee Goldstein et al., "The Effect of Transcendental Meditation on Self-Efficacy, Perceived Stress, and Quality of Life in Mothers in Uganda," *Health Care for Women International* 39(7) (July 2018): 734–54, doi.org/10.1080/07399332.2018.1445254.

N. Bregman-Hai and N. Soffer-Dudek, "Posttraumatic Symptoms and Poor Sleep Are Independent Pathways to Agency Disruptions and Dissociation: A Longitudinal Study with Objective Sleep Assessment," *Journal of Psychopathology and Clinical Science* 133(2) (February 2024): 192–207, doi.org/10.1037/abn0000885.

William D. S. Killgore et al., "Sleep Deprivation Reduces Perceived Emotional Intelligence and Constructive Thinking Skills," *Sleep Medicine* 9 (5) (July 2008): 517–26, doi.org/10.1016/j.sleep.2007.07.003.

David W. Hill, Jean E. Welch, and John A. Godfrey III, "Influence of Locus of Control on Mood State Disturbance After Short-Term Sleep Deprivation," *Sleep* 19 (1) (January 1996): 41–46, doi.org/10.1093/sleep/19.1.41.

PRINCIPLE 1: Put Connection First

3   **A close parent-child bond:** See Edith Chen, Gene H. Brody, and Gregory E. Miller, "Childhood Close Family Relationships and Health," *American Psychologist* 72, no. 6 (September 2017): 555–66, doi.org/10.1037/amp0000067. See also M. R. Gunnar et al., "Stress Reactivity and Attachment Security," *Developmental Psychobiology* 29 (3) (April 1996): 191–204, doi.org/10.1002/(SICI)1098-2302(199604)29:3<191::AID-DEV1>3.0.CO;2-M. See also Valarie King, Lisa Boyd, and Brianne Pragg, "Parent-Adolescent Closeness, Family Belonging, and Adolescent Well-Being Across Family Structures," *Journal of Family Issues* 39, no. 7 (2018): 2007–36, doi.org/10.1177/0192513X17739048. The power of close relationships with parents is also emphasized in Madeline Levine's excellent book *The Price of Privilege* (New York: HarperCollins, 2006), and by the relationship expert John Gottman in his book *Raising an Emotionally Intelligent Child* (New York: Simon & Schuster, 1997).

3   **In fact, one recent longitudinal:** Emma Freestone, "How Adolescents' Relationships with Their Parents Affect Mental Health," *BYU, College of Life Sciences, Public Health* (April 13, 2021), accessed June 18, 2024, ph.byu.edu/how-adolesecents-relationships-with-their-parents-affect-mental-health.

3   **And, even as parents everywhere:** Jonathan Rothwell, "Parenting Mitigates Social Media–Linked Mental Health Issues," *Gallup, Wellbeing* (October 27, 2023), accessed June 18, 2024, news.gallup.com/poll/513248/parenting-mitigates-social-media-linked-mental-health-issues.aspx.

8   **And the best part:** Mirjam Schneider, Irina Falkenberg, and Philipp Berger, "Parent-Child Play and the Emergence of External-

izing and Internalizing Behavior Problems in Childhood: A Systematic Review," *Frontiers in Psychology* 13 (May 2022), doi.org/10.3389/fpsyg.2022.822394.

11 **Not surprisingly, research has shown:** Jamie Ducharme, "'Phubbing' Is Hurting Your Relationships. Here's What It Is," *Time* (March 29, 2018), time.com/5216853/what-is-phubbing.

22 **Journalist Michaeleen Doucleff:** "I Was Constantly Arguing with My Child. Then I Learned the 'TEAM' Method of Calmer Parenting," *Time* (March 6, 2021), time.com/5944210/calm-parenting-technique.

PRINCIPLE 2: Be a Consultant, Not a Boss or Manager

27 **November might be a bit:** Imed Bouchrika, PhD, "College Dropout Rates: 2024 Statistics by Race, Gender & Income," Research.com (June 6, 2024), research.com/universities-colleges/college-dropout-rates#:~:text=Retention%20rate%20pertains%20to%20the,retention%20rate%20is%20about%2071%25.

PRINCIPLE 3: Communicate Healthy Expectations

61 **It's also been shown:** S. S. Luthar, N. L. Kumar, and N. Zillmer, "High-Achieving Schools Connote Risks for Adolescents: Problems Documented, Processes Implicated, and Directions for Interventions," *American Psychologist* 75(7) (2020): 983–95, doi.org/10.1037/amp0000556.

Mary B. Geisz and Mary Nakashian, "Adolescent Wellness: Current Perspectives and Future Opportunities in Research, Policy, and Practice: A Learning Report," Robert Wood Johnson Foundation (July 2018), rwjf.org/en/insights/our-research/2018/06/inspiring-and-powering-the-future--a-new-view-of-adolescence.html.

Thomas Curran and Andrew P. Hill, "Young People's Perceptions of Their Parents' Expectations and Criticism Are Increasing over Time: Implications for Perfectionism," *Psychological Bulletin* 148(1–2) (January–February 2022): 107–28, doi.org/10.1037/bul0000347.

66 **When a parent or a teacher:** Xitao Fan and Michael Chen, "Parental Involvement and Students' Academic Achievement: A

Meta-Analysis," *Educational Psychology Review* 13 (2001): 1–22, doi .org/10.1023/A:1009048817385. Also see William H. Jeynes, "Parental Involvement and Student Achievement: A Meta-Analysis," Harvard Family Research Project (2005), archive.globalfrp.org /publications-resources/publications-series/family-involvement -research-digests/parental-involvement-and-student-achievement-a -meta-analysis.

66 **For decades, we've known:** Renate Nummela Cain and Geoffrey Cain, *Making Connections: Teaching and the Human Brain,* rev. ed. (Boston: Addison-Wesley, 1994). Also see Virginia M. C. Tze, Lia M. Daniels, and Robert M. Klassen, "Evaluating the Relationship Between Boredom and Academic Outcomes: A Meta-Analysis," *Educational Psychology Review* 28 (March 2016): 119–44, doi.org/10.1007 /s10648-015-9301-y.

71 **While certainly some parents:** Stuart Slavin, Tawni Hoegland, MIchael Sorter, Nancy Eigel Miller, and Susan Shelton, "Depression, Anxiety, and Stressors in High Schol Students Prior to and During the Pandemic," to be published in *Education*.

90 **As we've said, research:** Andrew S. Quach et al., "Effects of Parental Warmth and Academic Pressure on Anxiety and Depression Symptoms in Chinese Adolescents," *Journal of Child and Family Studies* 24 (2015): 106–16, doi.org/10.1007/s10826-013-9818-y.

Zahra Hosseinkhani et al., "Academic Stress and Adolescents Mental Health: A Multilevel Structural Equation Modeling (MSEM) Study in Northwest of Iran," *Journal of Research in Health Sciences* 20(4) (October 31, 2020): e00496, doi: 10.34172/jrhs.2020.30.

PRINCIPLE 4: Teach Your Kids an Accurate Model of Reality

98 **Happy people obviously feel better:** Sonja Lyubomirsky, Laura King, and Ed Diener, "The Benefits of Frequent Positive Affect: Does Happiness Lead to Success?" *Psychological Bulletin* 131, no. 6 (November 2005): 803–55, doi.org/10.1037/0033-2909.131.6.803. See also Catherine A. Sanderson, *The Positive Shift: Mastering Mindset to Improve Happiness, Health, and Longevity* (Dallas, TX: BenBella Books, 2019).

100 And only eleven CEOs: Josh Moody, "Where the Top Fortune 500 CEOs Attended College," *U.S. News & World Report*, June 16, 2021, usnews.com/education/best-colleges/articles/where-the-top -fortune-500-ceos-attended-college.

101 For instance, a study: Lawrence S. Krieger and Kennon M. Sheldon, "What Makes Lawyers Happy? A Data-Driven Prescription to Redefine Professional Success," *George Washington Law Review* 83 (2015): 554–627, ir.law.fsu.edu/articles/94.

101 The disturbing statistic: Heather Stewart, "Physician Suicide: Contributing Factors and How to Prevent It," CHG Healthcare, March 29, 2023, chghealthcare.com/blog/physician -suicide-prevention.

102 Where you go to college: Stacy Berg Dale and Alan B. Krueger, "Estimating the Payoff to Attending a More Selective College: An Application of Selection on Observables and Unobservables," *Quarterly Journal of Economics* 117(4) (November 2002): 1491–1527, jstor .org/stable/4132484.

Julie Ray and Stephanie Marken, "Life in College Matters for Life After College," Gallup, May 6, 2014, gallup.com/poll/168848 /life-college-matters-life-college.aspx.

Anna Brown, "Public and Private College Grads Rank About Equally in Life Satisfaction," Pew Research Center, May 19, 2014, pewresearch.org/fact-tank/2014/05/19/public-and-private -college-grads-rank-about-equally-in-life-satisfaction.

102 Good relationships keep us healthier: Brooke C. Feeney and Roxanne L. Thrush, "Relationship Influences on Exploration in Adulthood: The Characteristics and Function of a Secure Base," *Journal of Personality and Social Psychology* 98, no. 1 (January 2010): 57–76, doi.org/10.1037/a0016961.

102 Money matters, but not nearly: Tim Kasser, *The High Price of Materialism* (Cambridge, MA: The MIT Press, 2002).

102 People succeed by devoting themselves: Khalid A. Bin Abdulrahman et al., "The Relationship Between Motivation and Academic Performance Among Medical Students in Riyadh," *Cureus* 15(10) (October 10, 2023): e46815, doi.org/10.7759/cureus.46815.

Lawrence S. Krieger and Kennon M. Sheldon, "What Makes Lawyers Happy?"

Marina S. Lemos and Lurdes Veríssimo, "The Relationships Between Intrinsic Motivation, Extrinsic Motivation, and Achievement, Along Elementary School," *Procedia—Social and Behavioral Sciences* 112 (February 7, 2014): 930–8, doi.org/10.1016/j.sbspro.2014.01.1251.

102 **We're actually not very good:** Daniel Gilbert, *Stumbling on Happiness* (New York: Alfred A. Knopf, 2006).

102 **Accomplishments matter:** Tim Kasser, *The High Price of Materialism.*

Edward L. Deci and Richard M. Ryan, *Intrinsic Motivation and Self-Determination in Human Behavior* (New York: Plenum, 1985).

Deci and Ryan, "The 'What' and 'Why' of Goal Pursuits: Human Needs and the Self-Determination of Behavior," *Psychological Inquiry* 11(4) (2000): 227–68, doi.org/10.1207/S15327965PLI1104_01.

Ryan and Deci, "Self-Determination Theory and the Facilitation of Intrinsic Motivation, Social Development, and Well-Being," *American Psychologist* 55(1) (2000): 68–78, doi.org/10.1037/0003-066X.55.1.68.

102 **Being happy—not "successful":** Lyubomirsky, King, and Diener, "The Benefits of Frequent Positive Affect." See also Catherine A. Sanderson, *The Positive Shift.*

107 **A class on happiness:** David Shimer, "Yale's Most Popular Class Ever: Happiness," January 2018, *The New York Times*, nytimes.com/2018/01/26/nyregion/at-yale-class-on-happiness-draws-huge-crowd-laurie-santos.html.

PRINCIPLE 6: Be a Nonanxious Presence in Your Family

152 **The Surgeon General issued:** The U.S. Surgeon General's Advisory on the Mental Health & Well-Being of Parents" chrome-extension://efaidnbmnnnibpcajpcglclefindmkaj/https://www.hhs.gov/sites/default/files/parents-under-pressure.pdf.

154 **Some umpires and referees:** Kerry Gillespie, "Physical Abuse, Extreme Verbal Assaults: Ontario Turns to Body Cameras to Help Save Youth Soccer Referees," *Toronto Star*, May 26, 2023, thestar.com/sports/soccer/physical-abuse-extreme-verbal-assaults-ontario-turns-to-body-cameras-to-help-save-youth-soccer/article_1c7a4d23-9680-5d27-aedc-32ce944dff01.html.

Kurt Schlosser, "High School Basketball Referees in Washington Are Using Body Cameras to Capture Unruly Behavior," GeekWire, January 20, 2024, geekwire.com/2024/high-school-basketball-ref erees-in-washington-are-using-body-cameras-to-capture-unruly -behavior/#:~:text=The%20body%20cameras%2C%20 which%20are,Unsportsmanlike%20technical%20foul.

156 **Take and score this test:** "Perceived Stress Scale," State of New Hampshire Employee Assistance Program, das.nh.gov/wellness /docs/percieved%20stress%20scale.pdf.

159 **Dr. Sonia Lupien:** "Recipe for Stress," Centre for Studies on Human Stress, humanstress.ca/stress/understand-your-stress/sources- of-stress.

PRINCIPLE 7: Encourage "Radical Downtime"

176 **Gloria Mark's studies:** Gloria Mark, Ph.D., *Attention Span: A Groundbreaking Way to Restore Balance, Happiness and Productivity* (New York: Hanover Square Books, 2023). See also: gloriamark.com /attention-span.

178 **we are not idle:** Mary Helen Immordino-Yang et al., "Rest Is Not Idleness: Implications of the Brain's Default Mode for Human De- velopment and Education," *Perspectives on Psychological Science* 7, no 4 (2012): doi.org/10.1177/1745691612447308.

189 **And the Centers for Disease:** "What Are Sleep Deprivation and Deficiency?," National Heart, Lung, and Blood Institute, nhlbi .nih.gov/health/sleep-deprivation#:~:text=According%20to%20 the%20Centers%20for,at%20least%20once%20a%20month.

194 **anxiety levels of medical professionals:** M. Nestor, A. Lawson, and D. Fischer "Improving the Mental Health and Well- Being of Healthcare Providers Using the Transcendental Med- itation Technique During the COVID-19 Pandemic: A Parallel Population Study." PlosOne 18(3) (March 3, 2023), doi: 10.1371 /journal.pone.0265046.

194 **medical students who practiced TM:** T. Nader et al., "A Larger Lens: Medical Students Benefit from Consciousness-Based Self-Care," in A. Maheshwari, *Consciousness-Based Leadership and Man- agement*, Vol. 2, 13–46, Online: Open Access August 18, 2023.

AN OVERLAPPING PRINCIPLE: Give Kids More Control in School

198 This is important stuff: Ellen Skinner and Teresa Greene, "Perceived Control, Coping, and Engagement," in *21st Century Education: A Reference Handbook*, ed. Thomas L. Good, vol. 1 (Thousand Oaks, CA: Sage Publications, 2008).

198 Moreover, athletics are reserved for: Juliana Menasce Horowitz and Nikki Graf, "Most U.S. Teens See Anxiety and Depression as a Major Problem Among Their Peers," Pew Research Center, February 20, 2019, pewresearch.org/social-trends/2019/02/20/most-u-s-teens-see-anxiety-and-depression-as-a-major-problem-among-their-peers.

200 A nationwide survey: Julia Moeller et al., "High School Students' Feelings: Discoveries from a Large National Survey and an Experience Sampling Study," *Learning and Instruction* 66 (April), doi.org/10.1016/j.learninstruc.2019.101301.

200 Although there are many sources: Suniya S. Luthar et al., "Students in High-Achieving Schools: Perils of Pressures to Be 'Standouts,'" *Adversity and Resilience Science* 1 (4) (June 2020): doi.org/10.1007/s42844-020-00009-3.

200 Student suicides are much lower: Tyler Black, "Children's Risk of Suicide Increases on School Days," *Scientific American*, August 22, 2022, scientificamerican.com/article/childrens-risk-of-suicide-increases-on-school-days.

200 There's currently a very high: Karissa Leduc et al., "School Refusal in Youth: A Systematic Review of Ecological Factors," *Child Psychiatry and Human Development* 55(4) (August 2024): 1044–1062, doi.org/10.1007/s10578-022-01469-7.

201 A high school student in Arizona: Donna St. George and Valerie Strauss, "The Crisis of Student Mental Health Is Much Vaster Than We Realize," *The Washington Post*, December 5, 2022.

203 It's no wonder that: From National Commission on Teaching and America's Future (NCTAF), according to U.S. Department of Education, "A National Conversation About Teaching." Also see Madeline Will, "5 Things to Know About Today's Teaching Force," EducationWeek, October 23, 2018, edweek.org/leadership/5-things-to-know-about-todays-teaching-force/2018/10.

Index

academic performance
  and autonomy of kids in school
    settings, 205
  effects of parental expectations, 63
  and expectations of parents, 67
  and meditation, 194
  and self-expectations, 72
  as source of stress, 200
  and student-directed learning, 207–8
accomplishments, 104, 107–13
accountability, 207
accurate model of reality, 98–118
achievement expectations, 63
addiction, 41, 52, 131
administrators (school), 202–3, 205, 208,
  213–14, 228
adolescents
  and autonomy of kids in school
    settings, 198
  and benefits of downtime, 175–76,
    191, 194, 195
  and benefits of sense of control, xviii
  effects of parental expectations, 61
  and emotional contagion, 153, 155
  and focus on college admissions, 98
  fostering confidence, 76
  fostering connection with, 11, 13
  and fostering connection with kids, 7
  and fostering self-development, 101
  impact of technology on brain
    development, xx
  and pressure to excel, xxv
  and substance use disorders, 104
alcohol use, 135–36
Alexander, Rianna, 201
ambivalence, 132–35
amygdala, xvii–xviii, 151, 152, 166,
  198, 210
anger, 137, 148, 151, 158
anorexia, 81
anxiety
  and benefits of downtime, 176–77
  and benefits of nonanxious presence,
    151–52, 155–71
  and brain physiology, xviii

  and consultant approach to parenting,
    39–40
  and emotional contagion, 152–55,
    170–71
  and lack of control, xvi–xvii
  managing as a parent, xxvi–xxvii
  and motivating kids, 136, 140–42
  and pitfalls of perfectionism, 81
  and pleasure vs. happiness, 106
  reacting to stressful situations, 147–52
  and school pressures, 147, 200–202
  and sleep requirements, 187, 189
  See also fear; stress
apologies, 161, 170
appetite, 187
assessment, 156–59. See also tests
athletics. See sports and athletics
attention-deficit/hyperactivity disorder
  (ADHD), 139
attitude, 189. See also mood
authoritarian parenting style, 37–39
authoritative parenting style, 37–39
autism, 139
autonomy
  and benefits of nonanxious presence,
    152, 163
  and consultant approach to parenting,
    44–45
  and cycle of stress in schools, 202–10
  of kids in school settings, 197–202,
    210–13, 215, 217
  and motivating kids, 125–26,
    128–29, 137
  and perceived stress, 157
  and self-advocacy at school, 218–25
  and sleep requirements, 192
  of teachers, 228
avoidance, 156

bedtime. See sleep habits
behaviors
  and discipline in school settings, 225–27
  and expectations of parents, 63
  and motivating kids, 128
  and myth of the good parent, 53

Bezos, Jeff, 99
body language, 13, 153
boundaries, 37, 193
boyd, danah, 43
brain development and physiology
  and autonomy of kids in school
    settings, 198, 210, 216, 228
  and benefits of nonanxious
    presence, 166
  and benefits of sense of control, xvii–xviii
  effects of anxiety, 151
  effects of autonomy on brain
    development, 45
  effects of gratification, 104
  and emotional contagion, 152
  and mistakes and failures, 86–87
  rate of brain development, 164
  See also amygdala; prefrontal cortex
burnout, 218

calculus, 215–16
calmness
  as benefit of sense of control, xv
  and benefits of nonanxious presence,
    xxvii, 151–52, 154, 160, 171
  and emotional contagion, 155
  and fostering connection with kids, 20
  practicing, xxviii
career choice, 64, 114
Centers for Disease Control and
  Prevention (CDC), 189, 208–9
Centre for Studies on Human Stress, 159
change
  "change talk," 135
  and motivating kids, 125–26, 132–37,
    137–42
choice, 212. See also autonomy
classroom assignments, 210–11
cleanliness, 53
coercion, 39
cognitive function, 194. See also brain
  development and physiology
college choice and admissions
  and achievement expectations of
    parents, 63

239

guidance, xxiv–xxv
guilt, 66, 137

habits
    and motivating kids, 128
    practicing calmness, xxix
    and preventive care, 166
    and responses to stress, 160
happiness and unhappiness
    and autonomy of kids in school
        settings, 228
    and benefits of nonanxious
        presence, 163
    and choosing a life that fits you, 114,
        116–17
    cycle of stress in schools, 209
    and cycle of stress in schools, 203
    and fostering self-development, 98,
        100–103
    and motivating kids, 123, 141
    and PERMA framework, 111–12
    and realistic view of the world, xxv–xxvi
    vs. pleasure, 104–9
health and hygiene skills, 30, 32
home-management skills, 31, 33
homework
    and autonomy of kids in school
        settings, 198, 204–6, 207–8, 213,
        214–15, 216, 217–18, 228
    and consultant approach to
        parenting, 50
    and motivating kids, 133
    and sleep requirements, 191
    as source of stress, 201, 202
    See also school work
Hunt, Gather, Parent (Doucleff), 22
hunter-gatherers, 22

identity, 178
Immordino-Yang, Mary Helen, 178
independence
    and challenges of college life, 27
    and consultant approach to
        parenting, 49
    and skills for leaving home, 27–28
    See also autonomy
individual attention, 10–12
infants, 151
insomnia, 190
interpersonal skills, 31, 33

jealousy, 23
judging parents, 54–56
judgment, 14–19, 20

Khan Academy, 212

Larson, Reed, 129
late bloomers, 101
Lew-Levy, Sheina, 22
listening skills, 6–7, 18, 20
Lupien, Sonia, 159
Lyubomirsky, Sonja, 102–3

marijuana use, 135–37
Mark, Gloria, 176

meaning and purpose, 107–13, 115, 122
medical school, 200, 209
medications, 27
meditation
    and autonomy of kids in school
        settings, 214
    and background of authors, iii
    and benefits of downtime, xxviii, 177,
        178, 193–96
    and benefits of nonanxious
        presence, 166
    and benefits of sense of control, xix
    and motivating kids, 140
    and PERMA framework, 108–9
    and pleasure vs. happiness, 105
melatonin supplements, 192
memory, 189, 194
mental health problems, 201–2, 209
mindfulness meditation, 194–95, 196
mind-wandering, xxviii, 177–86, 181–82,
        183–86. *See also* downtime
mirror neurons, 152
mistakes, 81, 84, 86–88. *See also* failure
modeling behaviors
    and benefits of nonanxious presence, 161
    and consultant approach to
        parenting, 49
    and meditation, 195
    and PERMA framework, 111
    and pitfalls of perfectionism, 86
    and sleep habits, 189
mood, 160, 187, 201. *See also* emotions
motivation
    challenges of, 121–25
    and change, 137–42
    and self-determination, 125–29,
        132–37
motivational interviewing, 135–37
multitasking, 176, 183
music, 183
The Myths of Happiness (Lyubomirsky),
        102–3

neuropsychology, 88
neuroscience, 199. *See also* brain
        development and physiology
neurotransmitters, 104
nonverbal language, 64
novelty, 159
N.U.T.S. framework, 159

objectivity, 49
obsessive-compulsive disorder, 81
Oettingen, Gabriele, 219
one-on-one time, 10–12
online learning programs, 212
online portals of schools, 217
OODA loop (Observe, Orient, Decide,
        Act), 21

pace of life, 175–76. *See also* schedules
paraphrasing, 20
parental behaviors, xx, 52–55
parent-child connection, 3–24
Perceived Stress Scale (PSS), 156–59
perfectionism, 61, 80–86

PERMA framework, 107–13
permissive parenting style, 37–39
personal space, 160–61
phones, 10–11
"phubbing," 11
physical health, 189
physiological self-control, xvii–xviii
play, 198
pleasure, 100–109, 104–5
police, 166
pop culture, 43. *See also* social media
positive emotion, 107–13
positive psychology, 107
positive self-talk, 76–77
practice, xxviii, 166–70
praise, 75, 77–78
prefrontal cortex
    and autonomy of kids in school
        settings, 210
    and benefits of nonanxious
        presence, 166
    and benefits of sense of control, xviii
    effects of anxiety, 151
    effects of autonomy on brain
        development, 45
    and emotional contagion, 152
    and focus, 87–88
    and sense of control, 198
    slow development of, 164
preventative care
    and benefits of nonanxious presence,
        151, 155–56, 165–66
    and benefits of sense of control, xviii
    and meditation, 195
    and motivating kids, 141
    and pleasure vs. happiness, 106
priorities, 91–92, 97–103
private time, 10–12. *See also* downtime
problem-solving skills, xxiv–xxv, 20,
        178, 215
productivity
    and autonomy of kids in school
        settings, 222
    and benefits of downtime, 176, 177,
        184–85
    and meditation, 194, 196
    and motivating kids, 138
    and sleep requirements, 187
protective instinct, 15–16, 22
psychotherapy, 61
public health crises, xvii
Putt, Jerry, 207, 218

quitting, 27, 38, 223

reassurance, 14, 15–16
recovery, 165–66
reflective listening, 20
relatedness, 125–26, 128–29
relationships
    and anxiety problems, 141–42
    and choosing a life that fits you, 115
    and cultivating calmness, 167–68
    and motivating kids, 126, 138
    and PERMA framework, 107–13
    and sleep requirements, 187, 191